MEDITERRANEO EDITIONS

Greek Cookery

200 Mediterranean flavours

TEXT & STYLING BY
STELLA KALOGERAKI

LAYOUT
VANGELIS PAPIOMYTOGLOU

DTP
NATASSA ANTONAKI

TRANSLATION
JILL PITTINGER

COPYRIGHT 2006
MEDITERRANEO EDITIONS
TEL. +3028310 21590, FAX: +3028310 21591

WWW.MEDITERRANEO.GR

ISBN: 960-8227-61-5

Greek
Cookery

200 Mediterranean flavours

CONTENTS

❧

MEAT AND MINCED MEAT

STARTERS
&
SALADS

Country salad

Wash the vegetables well and cut them into small pieces. Mix on a plate and add the feta, olives and oil. Season with salt and the salad is ready. A little oregano can also be scattered over the feta, for a stronger flavour.

1 tomato
1 cucumber
1 slice feta cheese
½ onion
Black olives
2-3 tbs olive oil
Salt

Skordalia

6 cloves of garlic
1 cup bread crusts
Salt
Juice of 1 lemon
2 tsp vinegar
1 cup olive oil

Pound the garlic in a mortar until it is well crushed. Add the salt and the bread, having first sprinkled the latter with a little water. Slowly, and alternately, add the oil, lemon and vinegar. Beat well until the skordalia acquires the preferred, soft consistency.

Dakos or Koukouvayia

Soak the rusk in water and then wrap it in a clean tea towel to dry. Mince the tomato and the feta and place on top of the rusk. Add the oil, salt, oregano and if liked, a little finely chopped onion.

1 barley rusk
1 tomato
1 slice feta cheese
2-3 tbs olive oil
Salt
1 onion
Oregano

Aubergine salad

Prick the aubergines with a fork and roast over charcoal or under a grill. When they are ready, remove the skins and puree the flesh in a blender. Add the lemon, salt, garlic and - slowly – the oil. Finally, if liked, add a few chopped walnuts.

1 kg round aubergines

1 cup olive oil

Juice of 1 lemon

2 crushed cloves of garlic

Salt

5-6 chopped walnuts (optional)

Taramosalata

Crumble the bread and place in a bowl with the taramas. Begin beating (use a mixer), and adding olive oil and lemon juice alternately in small quantities, until the mixture is soft and creamy. If liked, add a small amount of chopped walnuts and serve garnished with black olives.

150 gr taramas (fish roe)

300 gr stale bread

2 tbs lemon juice

1 cup olive oil

2-3 walnuts

Pickled artichokes

Clean the artichokes, cut into pieces if large, and place in a bowl with water and the lemon juice, to prevent them from discolouring. Prepare the pickling solution as follows: Add a whole egg to some water, and then begin to add salt until the egg rises to the surface and acquires a diameter the size of a 2 Euro piece. The solution is now ready. Add the cleaned artichokes and leave them covered for one day. On the following day drain off the solution, place the artichokes in a glass container and cover them with oil. Close the container well and store in a cool place. Serve with a little lemon juice or vinegar.

Little whole artichokes, or large ones cut into four

Olive oil

Vinegar

Salt

Lemon juice

1 kg strained
yogurt
1 large cucumber
5 cloves of garlic
1 bunch of dill
½ cup olive oil
Salt, pepper

Zatziki

Clean, grate and drain the cucumber. Pound the garlic in a mortar with the salt. In a bowl, mix together the yogurt, garlic, finely chopped dill, pepper and oil. Beat well in a mixer or by hand and the zatziki is ready. Cover and store in the refrigerator.

Piquant cheese
('tyrokafterí')

Mash the cheese. Roast the peppers, remove the skins and purée the flesh. Add to the cheese and very slowly add the olive oil, beating well. Finally, add the vinegar, beat to obtain a smooth purée, and it is ready to serve.

½ kg feta cheese
2 hot green peppers
½ cup olive oil
½ tbs vinegar

'Bouyourdi'

Place the feta in a small clay 'saganáki' (a small, round dish). Spread the tomatoes on top, then the slices of peppers and the oregano, and add a little oil. Bake for a short time in a moderate oven until the cheese has melted, and then serve hot in the dish.

300 gr feta cheese
3 slices of tomato
Oregano
Hot peppers
Olive oil

Oregano 'keftedes' from Pelion

Wash and peel the potatoes, boil them and then mash them to a purée. Add the taramás, the finely chopped onion, eggs, oregano and pepper, and mix well together. Place the mixture in the refrigerator for about 2 hours, and finally form into balls, roll them in flour and fry in very hot olive oil.

1 kg potatoes
150 gr taramás
(salted fish roe)
1 onion
2 eggs
1 tbs oregano
Pepper
Flour, and olive oil for frying

Salad of beetroot and yogurt

Clean the beetroot, wash them and boil them. When they are ready, strain well, keeping only the beets and discarding the stalks. Cut them into cubes. Add the yogurt, the mashed garlic, oil, salt and pepper. Mix well together and the salad is ready to serve!

1 kg beetroot
1 ½ kg strained yogurt
3 cloves garlic
1 small cup of oil
Salt, pepper

Aubergine croquettes

Wash the aubergines, roast them in the oven and remove the skins. Drain the flesh well and mash it in a bowl. Add the grated cheese, parsley, the finely chopped onion, baking powder, egg, and breadcrumbs (depending on the consistency of the mixture you may need to use little or more). Pour the other egg, beaten, on to a plate and have ready another plate of breadcrumbs. Form 'sausages' or balls from the mixture, dip them in the egg, roll them well in the breadcrumbs and fry in very hot oil.

1 kg aubergines
2 cups 'graviéra' cheese
1 tbs parsley
1 tsp onion
1 ½ tsp baking powder
1 egg
1 cup breadcrumbs
1 egg, and breadcrumbs for frying
Oil for frying

Potato croquettes

Boil the potatoes, peel them and mash to a purée. Add the butter, salt, grated cheese, egg yolks and breadcrumbs. Mix well and form into croquettes. Beat the egg and pour onto a plate, and have ready another plate of breadcrumbs. Dip the croquettes one by one in the egg and roll them in the breadcrumbs. Fry them in very hot oil until golden brown.

4 cups mashed
potato
4 tbs butter
1 tsp salt
1 ½ cups cheese
(feta and graviéra)
½ cup
breadcrumbs
2 egg yolks

1 egg. and
breadcrumbs for
frying
Oil for frying

Garlic macaroni, from Santorini

Pour the oil into a saucepan and as soon as it is hot, lightly sauté the finely chopped garlic. Add the chopped tomatoes, salt, pepper, sugar and rosemary. Lower the heat and leave the sauce to cook until the moisture has evaporated and it has thickened. Meanwhile, boil the macaroni in salted water, strain them, and rinse with cold water to prevent them from sticking together. Serve the macaroni on a plate surrounded by the sauce, and if desired, scatter over some cheese.

½ kg macaroni
4 tomatoes
4 cloves of garlic
½ tsp sugar
Small quantity of rosemary
Salt, pepper
½ cup oil

Potato salad

Boil the potatoes, peel them and cut them into cubes. Boil the vinegar together with the salt and pour it over the potatoes. Add the onions and finely chopped parsley. Dust with pepper and pour over the oil. Mix all well together and leave to rest in the refrigerator for 2-3 hours

1 kg potatoes
3 fresh spring onions
½ bunch of parsley
½ cup oil
½ cup vinegar
Salt, pepper

SAUCES

Oil and lemon dressing

1 cup olive oil

4 tbs lemon juice

½ tsp salt

1 tsp mustard (optional)

Mix together the ingredients and beat well; the sauce is ready. If a more piquant taste is desired, add 1 tsp mustard. Excellent with grilled or baked fish, vegetables or salads.

Egg and lemon (avgolemono)

Beat the eggs and very slowly add the lemon juice. Continue to beat while gradually adding some of the liquid. Finally, add the sauce to the pan containing the food and shake it so that the sauce is distributed around it.

2 eggs

Juice of two lemons

1-2 cups of liquid from the dish you are making

Oil and vinegar dressing

Mix together the ingredients and beat well. The sauce is ready. Use with salads or boiled vegetables.

> 1 cup olive oil
> ½ cup vinegar
> Salt

Béchamel

> 3 cups milk
> 3 tbs butter
> 7 tbs flour or cornflour
> Salt, pepper, nutmeg
> 2 eggs

Gently warm the milk. Place the butter in a pan and when it has just melted, add the flour. Mix well together and continue to beat while beginning to add the milk. Add the salt, pepper and nutmeg and stir over the heat until the sauce thickens and is smooth in consistency. When it has cooled slightly, add the eggs and beat well again.

Mayonnaise

Break the eggs, place the yolks in a bowl with the salt and beat well. (If beating by hand, care should be taken always to beat in the same direction). Now slowly add oil, beating at intervals. When nearly half the oil has been added, begin to add small amounts of oil and lemon juice alternately. As soon as the mayonnaise is thick, pour it into a glass bowl and store in the refrigerator. An excellent accompaniment to fish.

1 litre olive oil
1/2 cup lemon juice
4 egg yolks
1 tsp salt

PIES

Spinach pie

Clean the spinach and the leeks, and cut them up. Finely chop the dill and the onions. Heat the oil in a pan and sauti together the onions, leeks, dill and spinach. Add the salt and pepper, reduce the heat and leave for a few minutes to soften, without adding water. Remove the pan from the heat and when the mixture is cold, add the crumbled feta and the beaten eggs. Make the pastry as follows: place the flour in a bowl, make a well in the centre, and add the salt, oil, vinegar and (gradually) water to make a smooth dough. Form into a ball, cover and leave to rest for ½-1 hour. Then divide into four pieces and roll out into evenly-sized, thin sheets. Place one of these in a baking dish, the base and sides of which have been oiled. Brush the surface of the sheet with oil and add another piece of pastry. Now add the filling on top of the pastry, and cover with the two remaining sheets, oiling the surface of each. Press together the edges of the upper and lower sheets to seal. Brush with oil, sprinkle over the sesame and bake in a preheated oven for about 1 hour.

Pastry:
½ kg flour
½ cup olive oil
1 cup water
1 tsp salt
2 tbs vinegar
Sesame

Filling:
1 kg spinach
2 leeks
4 fresh spring onions
1 bunch dill
3 eggs
250 gr feta
Salt, pepper
1 cup olive oil

Cheese pie

Mix together the ingredients for the pastry and form the dough into a ball; cover and leave for a little while 'to rest'. Prepare the filling by mixing all the ingredients (except for one egg) together in a bowl. Now divide the pastry into two pieces and roll them out into two sheets. Lay one sheet in an oiled baking dish so that it extends up the sides, place the filling on top and then lay the other sheet of pastry over it. Press the two sheets well together to close the pie, brush the top with the remaining beaten egg and place the dish in a preheated oven. Leave to bake for about 1 hour.

Fyllo pastry:
1/2 kg flour
1 carton of yogurt
1 cup butter or oil

Filling:
1/2 kg feta cheese
3 eggs
1 cup milk
3 tbs flour
or semolina
2 tbs olive oil

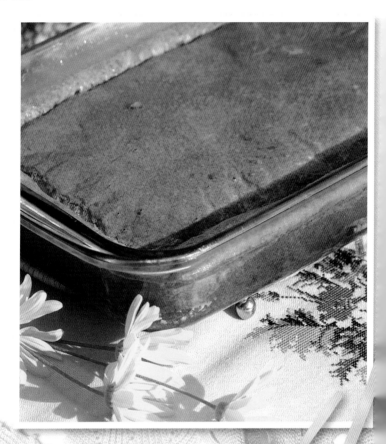

Cheese pie without pastry

Beat the butter well in your mixer and continue beating as you add the eggs. Add the remaining ingredients and mix together well. Oil a baking dish and pour the mixture into it – it should have a depth of about 3 cms. Bake in a preheated oven for about an hour.

½ kg feta cheese
1 cup grated graviera cheese
6 eggs
1 small tub of yogurt
200 gr butter
1 cup flour
2 tsp baking powder

Cheese pie from Skópelos

Put the flour in a bowl, add the salt, mix well and open a well in the centre. Pour in the oil and begin to mix together, adding warm water very slowly, until a medium-textured dough is formed. When ready, allow the dough to 'rest' for half an hour and then divide it into three balls. Take each one and roll out to a very thin sheet. Brush with oil and crumble 1/3 of the feta onto each sheet. Roll the sheets up into cylinders and then twist to form spirals. Bring plenty of oil to a high heat in a frying pan and fry the pies until they are golden brown.

½ kg flour
½ kg feta cheese
½ tsp salt
2 tbs olive oil
Warm water
Oil for frying

Leek pie

Prepare the pastry (as for spinach pie)
and let it rest. Wash and chop the leeks. Mix
well together in a bowl with the crumbled
feta, beaten eggs, milk, oil, salt and pepper.
Make four sheets of pastry and place two
in a baking dish, then add the filling and
place two sheets on top as in the previous
recipe. Brush the top of the pie with a
beaten egg and bake in a preheated oven
for about 1 hour.

Pastry:
½ kg flour
½ cup olive oil
1 cup water
1 tsp salt
2 tbs vinegar
Sesame

Filling:
1 kg leeks
6 eggs
300 gr feta
2 cups milk
Salt, pepper
½ cup olive oil

Leek and egg pie from Zagorohória

Clean and wash the leeks and cut them into small pieces. Add the boiled rice, grated cheeses, beaten eggs, yogurt, milk, and half of the oil. Prepare the pastry as follows: Place the flour in a large bowl, open a well in the centre and add the oil, vinegar and salt. Mix well to a medium dough with as much water as needed. Roll the pastry out into three sheets. Brush a baking dish with oil and butter and place the first sheet in it. Brush it with oil and butter and add half of the filling. Repeat with the second sheet of pastry and the remainder of the filling. Cover the pie with the third sheet, brushing it with oil, butter and a little milk. Bake the pie in a preheated oven for about 1 hour.

For the filling:
1 kg leeks
1 litre milk
1 small tub of yogurt
1 cup rice
6 eggs
500 gr feta and graviera cheese
3 cups olive oil and butter
2 tsp salt

For the pastry:
1 kg flour
3 tbs olive oil
1 tbs vinegar
Salt
Water as required
A little milk

Chicken pie, from Ioannina

Prepare the pastry as follows: put the flour into a bowl, open a well in the centre and add the oil and salt. Mix to a dough, gradually adding water, until a soft dough is formed which is not sticky. Divide it into three balls and leave them to 'rest' for a while. Heat the butter in a saucepan and sauté the finely chopped onion and the chicken cut into little pieces. Add the milk, rice, salt, and pepper and leave to boil until the rice is cooked. Remove from the heat and allow the mixture to cool well, so that the beaten eggs can be added without their cooking. Roll out the dough into three sheets. Butter the baking dish and put in one sheet, which should also be buttered, and place the second sheet on top. Spread the filling over it and cover with the third sheet of pastry. Brush the surface with oil and sprinkle over a little milk. Bake the pie in the oven for about one hour, until it is well browned.

1 free-range chicken
1 cup butter
1 large onion
1 cup rice
1 cup milk
5 eggs
Salt, pepper

For the pastry:
½ kg flour
2 small cups oli
oil
A little salt
Water

Minced beef pie

Make the pastry as follows: place the flour in a bowl, make a well in the centre, and add the salt, oil, vinegar and (gradually) water to make a smooth dough. Form into a ball, cover and leave to rest for ½-1 hour. Meanwhile, make the filling: heat the oil in a pan and sauté the finely chopped onions. Add the minced beef and stir constantly. Add a cup of water, the salt, pepper and nutmeg and allow to boil. When the meat is done, remove from the heat and after it has cooled add the cheese, the egg yolks, and the well-beaten whites. Stir well together. Cut the pastry into four pieces and roll them out into four thin sheets, two of which should be slightly larger. Oil the base and sides of a baking dish and line it with the two larger sheets, oiling the surface of each. Add the filling and cover with the two remaining sheets, which have also been oiled. Press together the edges of the upper and lower sheets to seal, score the surface into portions, brush with oil and bake in a preheated oven for about 1 hour.

Pastry:
½ kg flour
½ cup olive oil
1 cup water
1 tsp salt
2 tbs vinegar
Sesame

Filling:
1 kg minced beef
4 onions
1 cup grated parmesan cheese
4 eggs
salt, pepper, nutmeg
½ cup olive oil

Easter meat pie

Cut up the meat, wash and drain it, and then season with salt and pepper. Leave to marinate for one hour sprinkled with the lemon juice. Now simmer it in a saucepan over a low heat for about ½ hour. Remove from the heat and strain. Mix the cheeses in a separate bowl. Finely chop the mint. Make the pastry as follows: Sieve the flour together with the salt into a bowl and make a little well in the centre. Dissolve the yeast in a little warm water and add to the flour together with the egg and the milk. Mix into a firm dough, cover, and leave in a warm place. When the dough has risen, divide it into two and roll out into two sheets. Place one into an oiled baking dish so that it covers the sides and hangs over the edges. Now add the filling as follows: a layer of meat, a layer of cheese, then the mint (if desired, the fillings can be divided into two and this procedure carried out twice). Pour over the staka (thick cream) and cover with the second sheet of pastry. Wet your fingers and join the edges of the upper and lower sheet, pressing together the overhang and the top sheet to form a good seal. Brush the pie with beaten egg, sprinkle with sesame and bake in a preheated oven at 190 C for about ½ hour, until the pie has browned.

Filling:
1 ½ kg lamb
½ kg myzithra or anthotyro cheese
300 gr soft curd cheese
3 tbs finely chopped mint
4 tbs staka (thick cream)
Juice of 1 lemon
Salt, pepper

Pastry:
½ kg flour
1 envelope yeast
1 cup milk
1 egg
Pinch of salt

Courgette pie

Filling:

1 ½ kg green courgettes

½ kg feta

½ kg cream cheese

5 eggs, lightly beaten

A few mint leaves

Salt

Pastry:

½ kg flour

1 cup margarine

1 cup yogurt

Grate the courgettes, sprinkle them with salt and leave them in a sieve to drain. Press out the water from them with your hands. Meanwhile, crumble the cheese and mix together with the beaten eggs.

Mix together the courgettes with the cheese, finely chop and add the mint. Make the pastry as follows: beat together the margarine and yogurt in a bowl and add the flour. Knead into a dough suitable for rolling out into sheets. Form the dough into a ball, cover with a tea towel and leave to rest for ½ hour.

Divide the dough into two parts, one a little larger. Roll out into two sheets and spread the larger of the two in a buttered or oiled baking dish, so that the pastry covers the sides of the dish and hangs over. Spread the filling on top of the pastry and cover with the second sheet, pressing together the top and bottom sheets to seal. Oil the surface, score it and sprinkle over the sesame. Bake the pie in a moderate oven until the surface is well-browned.

'Galatópita' (milk pie) with macaroni, from Lefkáda

Boil the macaroni, strain them and leave aside. Retain one cup of milk and boil the rest in a saucepan. Dissolve the cornflour in the cup of milk which was set aside, and then add the mixture to the pan. Stir with a wooden spoon until the mixture has thickened. Remove from the heat and, stirring continuously, add the butter, sugar, cinnamon, clove and beaten eggs.
Butter a dish and tip the macaroni into it. Pour over the milk mixture, and bake at 180 C for about 1 hour.

1 ½ litres milk
4 eggs
100 gr thin macaroni
100 gr cornflour
1 cup sugar
1 tbs butter
Cinnamon, clove

Little pies filled with wild greens, fried

Filling:
1 kg wild greens
(or spinach)
1 bunch dill
4 fresh spring
onions
½ cup oil
Salt, pepper

Pastry:
½ kg flour
1 cup water
3 tbs oil
2 tbs lemon juice
Salt
Oil for frying

Wash the greens, dill and onions well and chop them. Place the oil in a pan and as soon as it has heated sauti the onions. Add the dill, greens, salt, pepper and two cups of water. Cover the pan and let the mixture cook for about ½ hour. When it is ready, transfer to a sieve and leave to drain well.

Meanwhile make the pastry as follows: place the flour with the salt in a bowl and make a well in the centre. Add the oil and lemon juice and mix together, adding water slowly to form an even, moderately soft dough. Shape into a ball, cover with a cloth and leave to rest for ½ hour. Thereafter, roll out into a very thin sheet and use a glass with a diameter of about 8 cms to cut out rounds. Place 1 tbs of the greens on each round and fold over the pastry to form a half-moon shape. Press together the edges with a fork to seal them and fry the pastries in a generous amount of boiling oil, taking care to brown them on both sides. Remove from the pan and place on kitchen paper on a plate, in order to drain off the oil.

EGGS

Omelette with wild greens

Pick over the greens, wash them well and boil them in water to which a little salt has been added. When they are ready strain them, cut them into small pieces and mix together with the crumbled cheese. Heat the oil to a high temperature in the frying pan and add half of the eggs. When the mixture sets, spread the greens on top of it and then add the remaining eggs. Turn the omelette to cook well on both sides.

½ kg asparagus or sweet wild greens

5 eggs

250 gr crumbled feta cheese

Salt, pepper

Olive oil for frying

Fried eggs with tomato sauce

5 eggs

4-5 ripe tomatoes

250 gr feta or kefalotyri cheese

salt, pepper

olive oil for frying

Wash the tomatoes and pass them through a sieve. Place the oil in a frying pan and bring to a high temperature. Add the tomatoes, salt and pepper; allow to cook and form a sauce. Then add the cheese, grated, and the eggs, taking care not to break them. When the whites have set, the dish is ready. Remove from the heat and serve each egg with a little sauce.

Omelette with courgettes

Wash the courgettes, cut them into medium rounds and fry them. Place on kitchen paper to drain. Finely chop the onions, sautı them in a little oil and add the courgettes. Beat the eggs and add the milk and flour, stirring it into the mixture. Add the eggs to the pan, stir briefly, season well and cook the omelette well on both sides.

1 kg small courgettes
6 eggs
1 onion
Salt, pepper
2 tbs milk
2 tbs flour
Olive oil for frying

Omelette with eggs and tomatoes (strapatsada)

Wash the tomatoes and pass them through a sieve. Beat the eggs, mix together with the tomatoes and season well. Heat the oil to a high temperature in a pan and add the mixture. Stir well, and add the grated cheese when it has cooked.

1 kg tomatoes

5 eggs

Salt, pepper

½ cup feta cheese

½ cup oil

Omelette with artichokes

Wash and clean the artichokes and place them in a bowl of water to which lemon juice has been added so that they do not discolour. Then cut them into small pieces and cook them in a pan without oil, until they have softened a little. Now add the oil and sauti them well. Beat the eggs and add them to the pan. Season well and turn the omelette to cook it on both sides.

4 eggs

3 artichokes

1 lemon

Salt, pepper

Olive oil for frying

'Froutália', from Andros
(omelette with sausages and potatoes)

½ sausage (large)

1 potato

2 eggs

Mint

½ cup grated kefalotyri cheese

Olive oil

Salt, pepper

Cut the sausage into 10 thin rounds, and the potato into rounds about 1 cm thick. Fry them a little, to soften them. Beat the eggs and add the salt, pepper, mint and cheese. Pour the mixture into the frying pan with the sausage and potatoes, shake it to distribute the mixture everywhere and cook over the heat until the omelette is well done on both sides.

PULSES
&
RICE

Bean soup

Soak the beans in water overnight to soften them. Next morning, change the water and boil them for about 15 minutes. Change the water again and add the onions, celery and finely chopped green peppers, chopped tomatoes, salt, pepper and oil. Allow all to boil for 20 minutes and then add the carrots cut into rounds. Remove from the heat after about ½ hour, when the beans have cooked and the sauce has thickened.

½ kg beans
½ kg tomatoes
2 green peppers
2 carrots
2 onions
Celery
Salt, pepper
1 cup olive oil

Giant dried beans in the oven

Soak the beans in water overnight to soften them. The following morning, rinse them and put them to boil in a pan of water for half an hour. Finely chop the onion and sauté it in hot oil, then add the garlic, celery, tomatoes, sugar and 1 cup of water. Boil the sauce for about half an hour. Strain the beans, spread them in a dish and add the sauce together with salt and pepper. Bake in the oven for about 40 minutes.

½ kg giant dried beans
1 onion
1-2 cloves of garlic
1 bunch of celery
2 tomatoes
1 tsp sugar
Salt, pepper
1 cup olive oil

Lentils

After washing the lentils well,
boil them in a pan with water for
10 minutes. Strain off the liquid
and add fresh water to cover. Add
the finely chopped onion, puree,
salt and pepper, bay leaf and oil.
Leave to cook until the lentils
have softened and the sauce has
thickened.

½ kg lentils
2 tbs tomato puree
1 onion
1 bay leaf
Salt, pepper
1 cup olive oil

Lentils and rice

Place the lentils in a pan with just enough water to cover them and bring to the boil. Drain and add fresh water; as soon as the liquid boils again, add the rice and the salt and allow to cook. Gently fry the finely chopped onions and add them, with the oil, to the pan of rice and lentils. Stir well together and after a little while, when the mixture has thickened, remove it from the heat.

1 cup lentils
½ cup rice
medium onions
Salt
1 cup olive oil

Chickpeas

½ kg chickpeas
1 lemon
½ tsp baking soda
1 tbs flour
1 onion
Salt, pepper
1 cup olive oil

Soak the chickpeas in water overnight to soften them. Next day, drain them, sprinkle over the baking soda, shake well to mix and leave them for half an hour. Then rinse them with abundant warm water and put them in a pan with water to boil, along with the oil, whole onion, salt and pepper. Leave over a low heat until they are left together with the oil. Shortly before removing them from the heat, add the lemon juice and the flour and let them boil a couple of times.

Chickpea fritters

Soak the chickpeas in water overnight
to soften them. Next day, drain them,
sprinkle over the baking soda, shake well
to mix and leave them for half an hour.
Then rinse them with abundant warm
water and put them in a pan with water
to boil, along with the oil, whole onion,
salt and pepper, until they are very soft.
Remove from the heat, strain them and
mash them to a puree. Add to this the
flour, onions, garlic and finely chopped
dill, form the mixture into fritters and fry
in very hot oil.

1 ½ cups chickpeas
½ cup flour
4 fresh spring onions
3 cloves of garlic
1 bunch of dill
1 tsp baking soda
Salt, pepper
Oil for frying

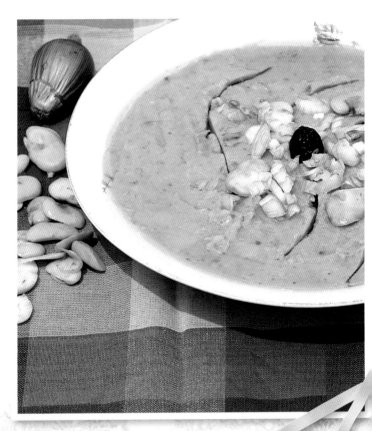

Dried broad beans

Soak the dried broad beans in water
overnight to soften them. Next day,
rinse them and boil for about half an
hour. Remove from the heat and strain.
When they are cooled, remove the skins
and throw them into a pan containing 2
cups of water and salt. When they have
softened and absorbed the water, remove
them from the heat. Pour over fresh
olive oil and serve garnished with finely
chopped spring onion.

½ kg dried broad
beans

1 onion

1 cup olive oil

Pilaf with saffron, from Kozani

2 cups risotto rice

5 tbs butter

30-40 strands of saffron

1/2 litre water or (meat stock)

Salt

Put the rice into a bowl and add hot water to cover. Stir well and leave for 10 minutes to soften, then wash the rice and drain it well. Put the butter into a saucepan and as soon as it begins to boil, sauté the rice. Then add the water or meat stock, the saffron and the salt. Cover the pan and leave the rice to boil until all the liquid has been absorbed.

VEGETABLES

Beetroots

Beetroots

Oil

Vinegar

Clean the beetroots and boil them whole in a generous amount of salted water. When they are soft, drain and cut into rounds or into four quarters along their vertical axis. Place in a bowl and add a mixture of oil and vinegar so that they are almost covered.

Green beans

1 kg fresh green beans

1/2 kg tomatoes

1 onion

1 cup olive oil

1-2 potatoes (optional)

Salt, pepper

Prepare the beans and wash them well. Sauté the onion and then add the beans. Add the chopped tomatoes, salt and pepper, and 1 cup of water. Leave to simmer over a medium heat for about 45 minutes. If liked, add two potatoes, cut into medium slices, after about 20 minutes.

Okra

repare the okra, wash and drain them,
hen sprinkle them with vinegar and
alt. Heat the oil in a pan and sauté the
nion; before it begins to brown, add
he chopped tomatoes and the pepper.
When the sauce begins to boil, add
he okra and, if necessary, a little
ater. Cook for about 30 minutes.

1 kg okra
1 cup oil
1 medium onion
2-3 tomatoes
Vinegar
Salt and pepper

Stuffed vegetables

Blanch the vine leaves, and wash and finely chop the herbs. Carefully scoop out the centres of the tomatoes, potatoes, aubergines and courgettes, leaving only the shell. Put the contents of the tomatoes into a bowl, to use in the filling. Add to this the finely chopped herbs, the grated onion, the rice, ½ cup of oil, a little of the water from the vine leaves and salt. Place the shells of the vegetables in a dish and fill them with the mixture, taking care that they are not filled to the top (otherwise the rice will expand and then overflow). Carefully roll up the same mixture in the vine leaves, so that it cannot escape from the edges, and also use it to stuff the courgette flowers. If there is any mixture left over add it around the vegetables, pour in the remainder of the oil and water, and bake in the oven.

800 gr rice for the filling
300 gr vine leaves
5 ripe tomatoes
5 peppers
5 courgettes
3 round aubergines
3 round potatoes
10 courgette flowers
3 onions

A few mint leaves
1 bunch parsley
1 bunch dill
2 cups oil
Salt, pepper

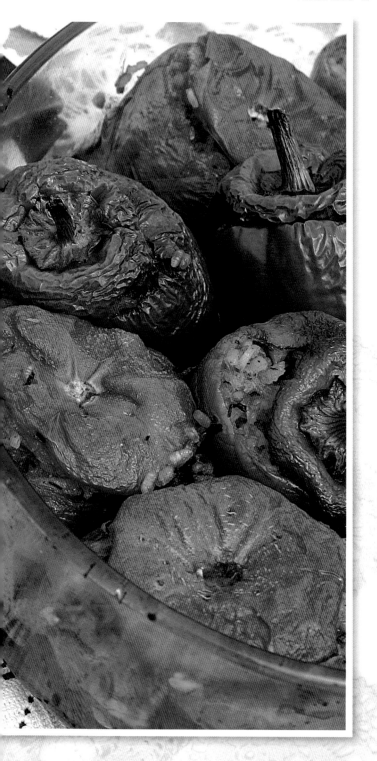

Stuffed courgette flowers

Carefully wash the flowers and cut out th
stigma from the centre. Finely chop th
onions, the garlic, dill, parsley and mi
and put them in a bowl with the rice an
oil. Season well. With a small spoon, fill th
flowers with the mixture, taking care tha
the mixture does not come right to the to
Close the flowers and place them in a pa
with the closed side downwards. Cover th
flowers with an inverted plate, to keep the
immobile while they are simmering. Ad
enough water to cover and cook for half a
hour until the rice has absorbed the wate
and only the flowers with their oil remai

20 courgette
flowers

½ kg rice for
filling

5 onions

2-3 cloves of garlic

1 bunch dill

1 bunch parsley

A few mint leaves

Salt, pepper

1 cup olive oil

'Soufikó', from Ikaria

Cut the aubergines into slices, salt them
and leave them to exude their bitter
juices for about half an hour. Then flour
them, put one cup of oil into a pan and
fry them. Arrange the slices in a baking
dish and spread the tomatoes, onion
and garlic, all finely chopped. Season,
add the remaining oil and then scatter
over the cheese, cut into cubes. Place
in the oven and bake for about ¾ hour.

1 kg aubergines

3 tomatoes

1 onion

2 cloves of garlic

250 gr feta cheese

1 cup flour

2 cups olive oil

Salt, pepper

Briam

repare the vegetables and wash them well;
ut them into slices, season with salt and
pread them out in a baking dish. Finely chop
he onions, garlic, parsley and tomatoes.
eason and add to the dish. Add the oil and
ne cup of water. If liked, scatter over pieces
f feta or another salty cheese. Bake in a
noderate oven for about one hour.

3 aubergines

4-5 courgettes

4-5 tomatoes

2 onions

2 cloves of garlic

2 green peppers

Finely chopped
parsley

2 cups olive oil

Salt, pepper

Salty cheese
(optional)

Spinach rice

Prepare and wash the spinach. Sauti the finely chopped onion in very hot oil and then add the dill and spinach, cooking it until it wilts. Add 1 cup of water and as soon as the mixture comes to the boil, add the rice; season well and allow to cook. Then remove from the heat and serve hot with lemon.

1 kg spinach
1 cup rice
1 onion
1 bunch of dill
Salt, pepper
1 cup olive oil

Cabbage rice

Bring the oil to a high temperature in a pan and sauti the finely chopped onion. Shred the cabbage and add to the onion in the pan, stir well and then add 1 cup of water and the lemon juice. When the mixture boils, add the rice and one more cup of water. Season well, reduce the heat and leave to boil for about 15 minutes, until a thickish sauce remains.

1 medium-sized cabbage
1 onion
½ cup rice
Juice of 1 lemon
Salt, pepper
½ cup olive oil

Courgette 'boreki'

Prepare and wash the vegetables. Cut the potatoes and courgettes into rounds with a thickness of about 1 cm and place them in separate bowls. Mash the cheese. Chop the tomatoes and add to the courgettes along with the finely chopped mint, salt and pepper, and mix well. Spread half of the potatoes in an oiled dish and then add a total of three alternating layers of the cheese and the courgette mixture. Finally, scatter over the remaining potatoes and sprinkle them with oregano. Pour over the oil and place in a preheated oven. Bake for about one hour, at first at a high temperature, and then reduce to a lower one.

½ kg courgettes

½ kg potatoes

2 large tomatoes

400 gr myzithra cheese

½ cup olive oil

A few mint leaves

½ tsp oregano

Salt and pepper

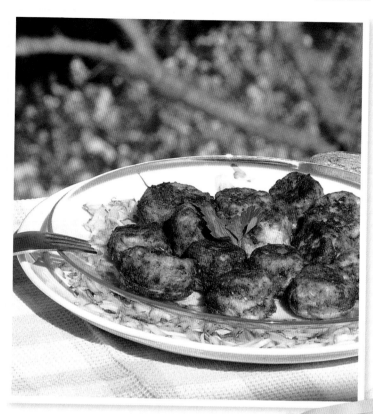

Courgette fritters

Wash the courgettes and grate them; sprinkle with salt and leave to drain. Then place them in a bowl with the crumbled feta cheese, breadcrumbs, beaten eggs, finely chopped parsley and pepper. Mix to a paste and then form into round fritters. Dip in flour and fry in very hot oil.

1 kg courgettes
1 cup flour
1 cup breadcrumbs
250 gr feta cheese
2 eggs
Parsley
Salt and pepper
Olive oil for frying

Fried aubergines with a red sauce

Wash the aubergines and cut them into slices, sprinkle with salt and leave them for about half an hour. Rinse them, drain well and then fry them. In another pan heat the oil, sautı the garlic and add the chopped tomatoes. Season with salt and pepper, add one cup of water and leave the sauce to simmer until it thickens. Place the fried aubergines in a dish, pour over the tomato sauce and bake in the oven for about 15-20 minutes.

1 kg aubergines

4-5 ripe tomatoes

4 cloves of garlic, finely chopped

Salt and pepper

½ cup olive oil

Aubergine rice with mint

Wash the aubergines, cut them into medium-sized cubes, sprinkle with salt and leave for an hour to sweeten. Put the oil into a pan and sautı the finely chopped onion. Add the aubergines, mix well and leave to cook on a low heat for 5 minutes. Add the finely chopped tomatoes or puree to the pan and after another five minutes, add 4 cups of water. As soon as the water begins to boil add the rice, mix well and leave to simmer for about 15 minutes. When it is ready, add the mint, turn off the heat and cover the pan with a clean tea towel for a short time, until the mint leaves have wilted.

1 kg elongated aubergines

1 ½ cups of rice

1 onion

2 tomatoes or 1 tbs puree

1 soup spoon fresh mint

1 cup olive oil

Salt, pepper

Aubergines Imam

Cut off the top of the aubergines, score them lengthwise, salt them and leave to drain for about 30 minutes. Rinse them, then cut them in half and fry them in very hot oil. When the flesh has softened, remove the aubergines from the pan with a slotted spoon and without breaking the skins scoop out the flesh with a spoon, keeping it separate. Gently sautı the onions in a pan with the garlic, cut into slices. Add the remaining ingredients (and the flesh of the aubergines) and allow them to soften. Place the aubergines in a dish and fill them with the mixture from the pan. If any filling is left over, pour it over the dish. Add a little oil and 1 cup of water and place the dish in a moderate oven for about half an hour.

4 aubergines
2 tomatoes
3 onions
4 cloves of garlic
½ bunch of parsley
Salt, pepper
1 cup olive oil

Fried aubergines

Wash the aubergines and cut them into rounds. Dip them one by one into a bowl containing beer. Drain well, season with salt and coat with flour. Heat olive oil in a frying pan to a high temperature and fry the aubergines. As soon as they are ready arrange the slices on a plate and scatter grated cheese over them.

1 kg round aubergines

3-4 tbs flour

Salt

Grated cheese

Beer

Oil for frying

Aubergine rolls with cheese

Cut the stalks off the aubergines, wash them and cut into slices. Place them in a bowl of water to sweeten. Meanwhile, prepare the sauce: sautı the onion in the oil, add the pureed tomatoes, salt, pepper and thyme and leave the sauce to cook. Drain the aubergines well, brush them with oil on the inside and spread 1 tsp of the crumbled feta on each. Roll them up and fasten with a toothpick to secure the ends. Arrange them in a dish, pour over the sauce and bake in the oven for about half and hour.

4 bottle-shaped aubergines

1 kg tomatoes

1 large onion

500 gr feta cheese

1 ½ cups olive oil

Salt, pepper, thyme

Boiled wild greens

Pick over the greens, chop them
and wash very carefully. Place a pan
containing a generous amount of water
on the heat and when it boils, add the
greens. After about 20 minutes they will
be cooked. Strain, season and serve hot
or cold with lemon, salt, and a generous
quantity of olive oil.

1 kg wild
greens
Salt
Lemon
Olive oil

Mushroom stew

Wash the mushrooms, cut off the stems and score them. Drain them, press out the water and if they are large cut them into smaller sections. Pour the oil into a pan and sauti the finely chopped onion together with the mushrooms. Add the chopped tomatoes, rosemary, salt and pepper. Cover and leave to cook over a low heat for about one hour. Meanwhile prepare the small onions; sauti them in a little oil, pour over the win and add the contents of the pan to the mushrooms. Allow to simme for about half an hour. Before turning off the heat, check to see if th mushrooms are still tough – if so, cook for a little longer.

1 kg flat
mushrooms

1 large onion

½ kg small
stewing onions

½ kg ripe tomatoe.

1 cup red wine

1 cup olive oil

½ cup rosemary

Salt, pepper

MEAT
&
MINCED MEAT

Rabbit in a red sauce

Wash the rabbit, cut it into pieces and
leave to drain. Heat the oil to a high
temperature in a pan and immediately
sauti the finely chopped onion with
the meat. Add the wine and then the
chopped tomatoes, salt, pepper and a
cup of water. Reduce the heat and leave
the meat to simmer. Check periodically
and, if necessary, add more water. When
the meat is tender and the sauce has
thickened, turn off the heat. Serve the
dish with fried potatoes

1 rabbit

1 onion

3-4 ripe tomatoes

1 cup oil

½ cup red wine

Salt, pepper

Rabbit or hare stew

Wash the rabbit or hare and cut it into pieces. Prepare the onions and push a clove into some of them. Sautı the meat in very hot oil and add the onions. Cover the pan for a few minutes, then remove the lid and add 1wineglass of red wine. Add the tomatoes, bay leaves, salt and pepper and 2 cups of water. Allow to simmer over a low heat for about one hour. Serve with fried potatoes.

. hare or 1 rabbit, 2.5 – 3 kg in weight

1 1/2 kg small onions

2-3 bay leaves

1 deep plateful of chopped tomatoes

2 cloves of garlic

A few cloves

1 glass red wine

1 cup olive oil

Salt, pepper

Rabbit with yogurt

Wash and drain the rabbit. Season well. Beat together the yogurt with the butter and fill the stomach cavity of the rabbit with it. Sew the stomach up tightly so that the mixture annot ooze out. Brush the rabbit with oil nd place in the oven. Roast for about 2 ours in a moderate oven, taking care to urn the rabbit occasionally so that it roasts rom all sides.

1 rabbit

1/2 kg yogurt

100 gr butter

Salt, pepper

Rabbit with artichokes

1 medium-sized
rabbit

10-12 artichokes

4 small onions

3 lemons

1 glass red wine

1 tbs flour

1 cup oil

Salt, pepper

Wash, drain and cut up the rabbit. Heat the oil in a pan and add the meat. Brown on all sides, turning frequently, and 'quench' with the red wine. Add the whole small onions, season, and then add a glass of water. Cover and leave to cook over a medium heat. Now clean and prepare the artichokes, leaving them whole if they are small and incising a cross into the base, or cutting them into two pieces if large. To prevent them from discolouring, place them in a bowl of water containing the juice of one lemon. About 15 minutes before the end of the roasting time, add the artichokes to the rabbit. As soon as they have softened, remove a little of the juices from the pan to a small bowl. Add the juice from the lemons, the flour and the water. Beat well and then pour the mixture into the pan and shake well to distribute the liquid. Allow the sauce to boil and as soon as it has thickened, remove from the heat.

Rooster with 'hylopites'

Wash the bird, cut into pieces and sauti in a little oil. As soon as it begins to brown, add the onion and stir together. Add the wine, salt, pepper, fresh tomatoes, oil and a little water. Allow to simmer until the meat is tender. Remove the meat from the pan, add the hylopites and boil in the liquid for about 15 minutes. Put the meat into a baking dish or clay pot, add the hylopites and the sun-dried tomatoes and cook in a moderate oven for about another 30 minutes. As soon as it is removed from the oven, sprinkle over the grated cheese.

500 gr hylopites

1 rooster, about 1 1/2 kg in weight

1 cup olive oil

1 finely chopped onion

2 cups chopped tomatoes

10 sun-dried tomatoes

1/2 cup red wine

Salt, pepper

Grated kefalotyri cheese

Chicken with peppers

Fry the chicken in the oil, having first tossed the pieces in a mixture of flour, salt, pepper and paprika. Remove the chicken with a slotted spoon and in the same oil sauti the onion, garlic, and peppers cut into small pieces. As soon as they have softened, add the tomato juice and leave the sauce to cook for a short time over a low heat. Now add the chicken, cover the pan and cook for about another thirty minutes.

1 chicken cut into portions

1 onion

1 clove of garlic

3 green peppers

3 red peppers

1 cup tomato juice

1 cup oil

1 cup flour

Salt, pepper, paprika

Chicken with 'trahanás or buckwheat, from Thrace

Boil the chicken in a large quantity of salted water. Strain, then put it into a baking dish. Retain the liquid separately. Put the oil into another pan and as soon as it is hot, sauté the finely chopped onion. Add the chopped tomatoes and bring the sauce to the boil a few times. Then add the liquid and as soon as it boils, add the 'trahanás (or buckwheat). Leave for a few minutes and then add it to the dish, distributing it around the chicken. Place in the oven and bake until the chicken and 'trahanás' or buckwheat are all browned.

1 chicken
3 cups 'trahanás, or buckwheat
1 onion
3 tomatoes
½ cup olive oil
Salt

Chicken in a red sauce

1 chicken
½ cup oil
4-5 ripe tomatoes
1 onion
1 tsp sugar
salt, pepper

Wash the chicken and cut into pieces; leave to drain. Pour the oil into a pan and as soon as it is hot, sautı the finely chopped onion and the meat. When it has browned add the tomatoes, crushed, the sugar, salt, pepper and one cup of water. Reduce the heat and leave to simmer gently until the meat is tender and left with a thickish sauce. This dish can be served with fried potatoes, rice or macaroni.

Chicken with piquant olives

Wash the chicken well, cut into portions, sprinkle with salt and leave to drain. Bring the oil to a high temperature in a pan and sauti the meat with the onions and garlic 'Quench' with the wine and add the chopped tomatoes, oregano, pepper a pinch of salt and 2 cups of water Leave to cook for about 45 minute and then add the olives from which you have removed the stones. Cook for a further 15 minutes

1 ½ kg chicken

4-5 ripe tomatoes

150 gr black olives preserved in vinegar

10 small onions

1 clove of garlic

1 cup wine

Oregano

1 cup oil

Salt, pepper

Chicken from Bardouna, Lakonia

Wash the chicken well, leave to drain, then cut it into portions and sauté it in oil until it is browned. Add the onions cut into rings, the tomato paste and 1 cup of water. Season, then cover the pan and leave the contents to cook over a low heat. About 10 minutes before the cooking is completed, add the olives and then the cheese cut into little pieces. Leave for a while until it has melted, and the dish is then ready to serve.

1 chicken

1 kg onions

250 gr green 'tsakistés' olives

½ kg kefalograviera cheese

1 tbs tomato paste

1 cup olive oil

Salt, pepper

Chicken with yogurt

Wash the chicken and cut into pieces, pour over the lemon juice and season, and leave in a bowl for 1 hour. Then place in a baking dish with the oil and a little water and bake in the oven. Beat the yogurt with the eggs and 2 tbs of water and when the chicken is ready, pour over the sauce. Return the dish to the oven for a short time, and then it is ready.

1 ½ kg chicken

½ kg yogurt

1 cup oil

2 lemons

2 eggs

Salt, pepper

A few breadcrumbs

'Coq au vin'

Wash the bird and cut into pieces. Sauti the finely chopped onion, garlic, and meat in hot oil. After a few minutes, 'quench' the meat with the wine and add the chopped tomatoes, salt, pepper and 2 cups of water. Leave to simmer over a low heat for about 1 hour. Serve with fried potatoes or rice.

1 rooster or chicken

1 onion

2 cloves of garlic

1 deep plate of chopped tomatoes

1 glass red wine

Salt, pepper

1 cup olive oil

Chicken with okra

Wash the chicken, cut it into pieces and leave to drain. Pour the oil into a pan and sauti the finely chopped onions with the meat. As soon as it has browned, add the chopped tomatoes, sugar, salt, pepper and 1 cup of water. Reduce the heat and leave to simmer. When the meat is tender remove it from the pan with a slotted spoon and arrange it on a plate. Now wash the okra, removing their caps, and fry them gently in very hot oil, in stages, until they brown. Then put them into the pan containing the sauce from the meat, add a little water and leave to cook over a low heat. Do not stir, as this would break up the okra. When they are ready, add them to the plate containing the chicken and pour any remaining sauce over the whole dish.

1 chicken
1 kg okra
½ cup oil
1 kg ripe tomatoes
2 onions
1 tsp sugar
salt, pepper

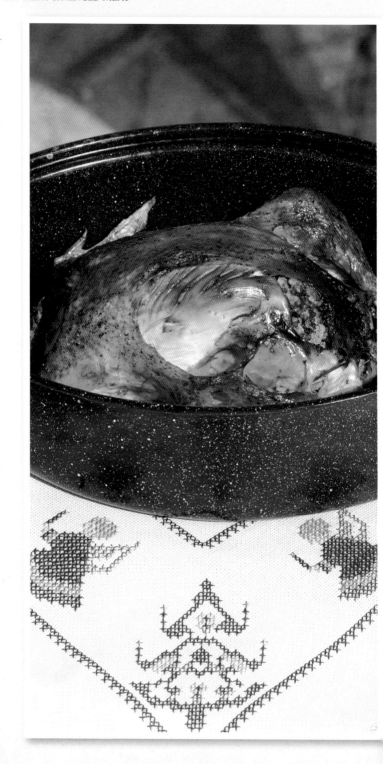

Stuffed turkey

turkey, 4-5 kg
in weight
1 onion
kg minced meat
(pork and beef)
250 gr ham
1 cup white wine
200 gr rice
80 gr raisins
100 gr pine nuts
100 gr apples
300 gr chestnuts
200 gr butter
1 cup red wine
Salt and pepper
Olive oil

Remove the giblets from the turkey, wash it and leave to drain. Finely chop the giblets and sauté them in a little oil with the minced meat, ham and finely chopped onion. 'Quench' with the white wine and add the raisins, pine nuts, rice and chopped apples. Cook for about 15 minutes and just before the end of the time, add the boiled chestnuts. Mix well together, then use it to stuff the turkey. Place the bird in a pot (crock) and bake in a preheated oven for about 2 hours, brushing it from time to time with the melted butter.

Pilaf with chicken livers

Wash the livers and boil them lightly in water. Strain well, and then sauté them in the oil with the finely chopped onion. 'Quench' with the wine and add the chopped tomatoes, salt and pepper. Leave for a while so that the livers are cooked and the sauce has thickened. Meanwhile, boil the rice in salted water. Serve simply, garnishing the rice with the livers and their sauce. If desired, the dish can be served from a mould in the following way:
Spread the livers and sauce on the bottom of the mould and add the rice on top. Invert the mould onto a plate to produce an attractive dish in which the moulded rice is decorated by the livers and sauce.

½ kg chicken
livers
1 onion
2 ripe tomatoes
½ kg rice
½ cup white wine
½ cup olive oil
Salt, pepper

Beef in a red sauce

Wash the beef and cut it into small pieces. Gently fry the finely chopped onion, garlic and meat in hot oil for a few minutes, then pour over the wine and add the tomato, bay leaf, clove, cinnamon, salt, pepper and 2 cups of water. Allow to simmer over a low heat for about 1 hour. Serve with fried potatoes, rice or boiled pasta.

1 kg beef

1 onion

2 cloves of garlic

1 kg chopped tomatoes

1-2 bay leaves

1 cinnamon stick

3-4 cloves

1 glass red wine

Salt, pepper

1 cup olive oil

'Pastitsáda,' from Corfu

Wash and drain the meat. Cut it into medium-sized pieces and sauté them in the oil. When they brown, add the onions and the finely chopped garlic and pour over the wine. Now add the finely chopped tomatoes, salt and pepper, bay leaf, cinnamon, clove, sugar and a little water, so that the meat is covered. Leave to cook over a low heat for 1½- 2 hours. Meanwhile, boil and strain the macaroni. When the meat is ready, add the macaroni to the sauce and serve hot with grated kefalotyri cheese sprinkled over it.

1 kg beef
1 cup olive oil
3 onions
2-3 cloves of garlic
½ cup white wine
½ tsp powdered cinnamon and clove
1 tsp paprika
1 tsp black pepper
1 bay leaf
½ kg tomatoes
½ kg macaroni
250 gr grated kefalotyri cheese
1 tsp sugar
Salt

'Sofríto', from Corfu

Wash, drain, cut up and flour the meat. Fry lightly and then remove from the pan. Pour a little oil into a saucepan and sauté the garlic and finely chopped parsley. 'Quench' with the wine and add the meat, bay leaves, salt and pepper and water, enough to cover the contents. Cover the saucepan and leave the meat to simmer. Serve, when ready, with mashed potatoes.

6-7 slices of beef (lean, with a thickness of 2 cms)
Flour for frying
1 cup olive oil
3-4 cloves of garlic
2 tbs parsley
2 bay leaves
1 small cup white wine
Salt, pepper

'Bekri Mezé'

1 kg beef
2 cups red wine
1 ½ cups tomato juice
3 cloves of garlic
1 onion
2 tbs mustard
Oregano
½ tsp allspice
½ cup oil
Salt, pepper

Wash the meat and cut it into chunks. Put them in a bowl with a little of the oil, the wine, mustard, oregano, allspice, salt and pepper. Mix well and leave to marinate overnight in the refrigerator. The following day, put the remaining oil into a pan and sauté the onion, garlic and meat. Add the marinating juices, tomato juice and one cup of water, and leave to cook over a low heat for about 2 hours. If necessary, add a little more water and cook until only the meat remains with its sauce.

Beef with macaroni

Wash the meat, cut it into pieces and leave for a while to drain. Heat the oil in a pan and sautі the finely chopped onion and the meat. As soon as the latter begins to brown, add the finely chopped tomatoes, salt, pepper, and 2 cups of water. Leave to simmer and shortly before it is ready add another 4 cups of water. When the liquid boils, add the macaroni and leave to cook until it is soft and there is only a little red sauce left in the pan.

1 kg beef
½ cup oil
1 onion
3-4 ripe tomatoes
½ kg macaroni
Salt, pepper

Beef with peas

Cut the meat into medium-sized pieces, wash and leave it to strain. Heat the oil to a very high temperature in a pan and gently fry the meat to brown it on all sides. Add the onions and continue to fry everything together. Add the chopped tomatoes, salt, and pepper, cover the pan and reduce the heat. When the meat is partly cooked, add the peas and a little water and leave to cook further until the meat is tender and the sauce thick.

1 kg beef

1kg peas

1 cup oil

1 onion

4-5 ripe tomatoes

1 bunch of dill

Salt, pepper

Beef with courgettes, egg and lemon

Cut the meat into medium-sized pieces, wash it and leave to drain. Heat the oil to a very high temperature in a pan and gently fry the meat to brown it on all sides. Add the onions and continue to fry everything together. Add 2 cups of water, salt, and pepper, cover the pan and leave the meat to cook over a low temperature. In the meantime, wash the courgettes and cut them into large pieces (leave whole if very small), and finely chop the dill. When the meat is half cooked, add the courgettes and dill to the pan. When everything is ready, turn off the heat and prepare the egg and lemon sauce as follows: beat the eggs well and without stopping, add the juice of the lemons and a little of the juices from the pan. Then pour the sauce over the meat and courgettes, shaking the pan so that it is well distributed, and serve.

1 kg beef
1 onion
1 cup oil
1 kg courgettes
1 bunch of dill
2 eggs
2 lemons
Salt, pepper

Beef with green olives

Wash the meat and cut into medium-sized pieces. Heat the oil in a pan and fry the meat until it browns. Add the chopped tomatoes, finely chopped garlic, cinnamon, salt and pepper and 1 cup of water. Leave to simmer for about 20 minutes. In the meantime, toss the green olives into scalding hot water and when the meat is half cooked, add them to the pan. Cook for about another half an hour.

1 kg beef
½ kg green olives
3-4 ripe tomatoes
1 clove of garlic
Cinnamon
Salt, pepper
1 cup olive oil

Beef with quinces

1 kg beef

1 kg quinces

1 onion

3 tbs tomato paste

1 tsp sugar

1 bay leaf

1 cinnamon stick

Salt, pepper

1 cup olive oil

Finely chop the onions and sautı them in half of the oil together with the meat cut into small pieces. Add 2 cups of water, the tomato paste, sugar, salt and pepper and leave to cook over a low heat for about half an hour. In the meantime wash the quinces, cut into thick slices and sautı them in a frying pan with a little oil. When the meat is almost cooked, transfer it to a baking dish, add the quinces, cinnamon and bay leaf, and place it in the oven to bake for a while.

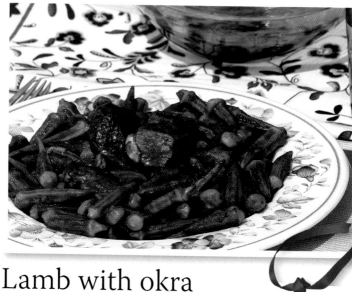

Lamb with okra

Wash the okra and lightly cut into their caps. Cut the meat into portions and sauté it in hot oil together with the finely chopped onion. Add the juice from the tomatoes to the pan and bring to the boil. Now add the okra, salt, pepper and 2 cups of water, and leave to cook over a low heat.

1 kg lamb
1 kg okra
½ kg tomatoes
1 onion
Salt, pepper
1 cup oil

Lamb youvetsi

Wash the meat, cut it into portions and place it in a baking dish. Add the tomatoes, onions and the finely chopped garlic, salt, pepper, oil and 1 cup of water. Bake in the oven and when the meat is almost cooked, add the 'kritharaki'.

1 kg lamb
½ kg 'kritharaki' (grain-sized pasta)
½ kg tomatoes
1 onion
1 whole garlic
1 cup olive oil
Salt, pepper

Lamb with courgettes

Wash the meat, cut into pieces, season it and roll in flour. Heat the oil in a pan and sautı the finely chopped onion together with the meat. Add the chopped tomatoes, finely chopped parsley, salt, pepper and 2 cups of water. Cover the pan and leave to cook for one hour. In the meantime wash the courgettes; cut them into medium-sized pieces or if they are very small, they may be left whole. Add to the meat in the pan and continuing cooking for about another half hour.

1 kg lamb
1kg courgettes
3-4 ripe tomatoes
1 onion
Parsley
2-3 tbs flour
Salt, pepper
1/2 cup olive oil

Lamb with hylopites

Cut the meat into cubes and sautı in very hot oil wit the finely chopped onion and garlic. Add the pepper and carrot. After another 2 minutes, add I cup of water and as soon as it boils remove the scum that forms with a slotted spoon. Leave the meat to simmer for about 1 hour. When it is half cooked, add the chopped tomatoes and seasonings. Add the hylopites and continue to cook for about another 20 minutes until the red sauce has thickened, the hylopites are cooked and the meat is tender. Serve hot, sprinkled with the grated cheese.

1 kg lamb

1 onion

½ clove of garlic

4 tbs oil

1 pepper

1 carrot

2 medium-sized tomatoes

½ kg hylopites

½ cup grated cheese

Salt, pepper

Lamb fricasée

Wash the meat, season and cut into portions. Heat the oil in a pan, sauté the onions which have previously been cut into thick chunks, and add the meat. When the meat is well fried, add ½ cup of water and bring to the boil. Wash and pick over the parsley (or lettuce), add it to the meat in the pan and season with salt and pepper. When the dish is ready, beat the eggs and without stopping, gradually add the lemon juice as well as a little of the liquid from the pan. Now add the egg and lemon sauce to the pan, shaking it well to distribute evenly, and the food is ready.

Lamb fricasée can be made with parsley or lettuce – the method is the same.

1 kg lamb

½ kg small onions

1 kg parsley or 3 lettuces

2 eggs

1 lemon

½ cup oil

salt, pepper

'Browned' lamb

Cut the meat into small pieces, wash
and leave to drain well. Heat the
oil in a pan and immediately add
the meat, salt and pepper. When it
begins to brown, reduce the heat,
cover the pan and leave the meat to
brown further in the oil (without
water) until it is tender.

1 kg lamb
4 tbs oil
Salt
pepper

'Psíma'
(Easter lamb from Halkidiki)

Wash the meat, cut it into portions and boil it for about half an hour in salted water. Meanwhile, sauté the onions and the dill in the butter, salt the mixture lightly and spread it out in a baking dish. Transfer the meat to the dish, placing it on top of the onions, add a little of the liquid from the pan in which it was cooked, and put the dish in the oven. When the meat is almost done, add 3 cups of water to the dish, the sultanas and the rice (making sure that they are beneath the meat) and put it back in the oven until the rice is cooked.

1 ½ kg lamb
(shoulder or leg)

½ kg spring
onions

1 ½ kg rice

1 ½ cups sultanas

2 cups butter

Dill

Salt, black pepper

Lamb with wheat, from Mytilene ('Keskék')

Wash the meat, cut it into thin slices, and boil it in salted water. In another pan boil the onions, cut into thick pieces. Add the wheat and the liquid from the meat. Stir well together and leave the wheat to cook. Meanwhile, remove any bones from the meat, cut it into very small pieces and put it into a casserole with the wheat. Pour over the oil, and place it over a low heat until it 'binds' and the cooking is completed.

1 kg lamb
1 kg hulled wheat
½ kg onions
Oil
Salt, pepper

'Frikadélia,' from Rouméli

Wash the caul and the livers well, and cut them into small pieces. Place the caul in water to which lemon juice has been added for about half an hour, in order to cleanse and 'whiten' it. Season the pieces of liver and dust them with oregano. Now take each piece separately and wrap it in a piece of caul. Close the 'packets' with toothpicks to prevent them from opening and arrange them in a dish. Sprinkle with oil, pour over the lemon juice and place the dish in the oven for about ¾ of an hour, until the caul is seen to have browned. If desired, serve with a sauce of oil and lemon

2 lambs' livers
1 lamb's caul
2 lemons
1 tbs oil
Oregano
Salt, pepper

'Regáli', from Mani

Wash the liver, blanch it for a few minutes in boiling water and then cut it into cubes. Put the oil in a pan and as soon as it is very hot, sauté the liver and the onions, finely chopped. 'Quench' with the wine and leave for about 4-5 minutes to boil. Add the tomato paste dissolved with 1 cup of water, the nutmeg, salt and pepper, and cook slowly until the liver is left with the liquid reduced to a sauce.

1 lamb's liver
¾ cup oil
2 onions
1 cup red wine
small quantity
of nutmeg
1 tbs tomato
paste
salt, pepper

'Kokorétsi'

1 lamb's liver
1 kg sweetbreads
1 lamb's caul
1 kg lambs'
intestines
1 lemon
salt, pepper,
oregano

Wash the intestines well, turning them inside out several times. Place in a bowl with the lemon juice and leave to one side. Wash the liver and sweetbreads well, cut them into small pieces and drain. Season, dust them with oregano and thread them one by one onto a spit. Now wrap the caul around them and finally bind them by winding the intestines tightly around them. Roast the 'kokorétsi' over charcoals, not forgetting to brush them from time to time with oil.

Lamb with yogurt

Wash the meat, season it with salt and leave it to marinate for one night in the refrigerator. Next day, wipe the meat, make some incisions into it and push slivers of garlic into them. Pour over the oil, scatter over pepper and thyme, and roast the lamb in the oven at 200 C. When it is ready, take the juices from the pan and beat them together with the yogurt and the beaten eggs. Remove the meat from the bone, and if liked, transfer it from the roasting tin to a more closed vessel, such as a clay pot. Pour over the yogurt sauce. Return the meat to the oven for about half an hour until the sauce has thickened and the yogurt has taken on a colour.

1 ½ kg leg of lamb

500 gr strained yogurt

2 eggs

1 lemon

2-3 cloves of garlic

½ cup oil

Thyme

Salt and pepper

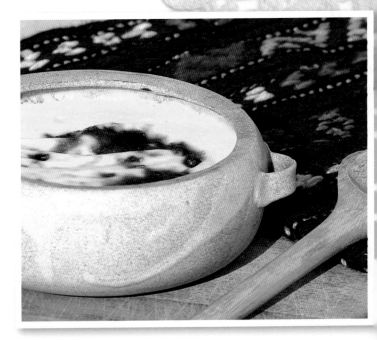

Lamb in a paper parcel

Wash the meat well, drain it and then score it lightly at intervals. Push a small piece of garlic and a little sprig of rosemary into the incisions. Place the leg of lamb on two sheets of greaseproof paper. Brush with oil, pour over the lemon juice, and season. Wrap the meat in the paper and place the parcel on top of two other sheets, wrapping them in the opposite direction – the aim is to close the packet well on all sides, so that the moisture cannot escape. Place in a dish and bake in a moderate oven for about 3 hours.

1 leg of lamb
(about 2 kg in
weight)
3 cloves of garlic
Rosemary
2 lemons
4 tbs olive oil
Salt, pepper

'Gardoúba,' from Roúmeli

Wash the intestines very carefully, turning them inside out several times. When they are very clean, place them in a bowl with vinegar. Leave for a while, then rinse and allow them to drain. Wash the offal with equal care and cut it into elongated pieces. Use the intestines to wrap the offal and form little 'gardoubákia'. Arrange them in a baking dish and add the onions and dill, finely chopped, the tomato juice, oil and salt and pepper. Bake in the oven for about 1 hour.

1 1/2 kg lambs'
intestines
1 kg lambs'
offal (livers,
sweetbreads etc.)
3-4 spring
onions
Dill
1 cup tomato
juice
1/2 cup olive oil
Vinegar

Lamb with avronies

Cut up the meat, wash and drain it, and fry it in very hot oil until it is browned, adding the finely chopped onion towards the end. When the onion has softened, season well and add one cup of water. Cover the pan and leave to cook on a low heat. In the meantime, prepare, wash and cut up the avronies. When the meat is cooked, take it from the pan with a slotted spoon and set aside. Place the stalks of the avronies in the pan with a little water. When they are partly cooked add the tips, season and leave to cook further. Finally, dissolve 1 tbs of flour in the juice of 1 lemon, add it to the pan and shake to distribute it. Add the meat and bring all to the boil, when the sauce will thicken.

1 kg lamb
1 onion
1 kg avronies
1 lemon
Salt, pepper
2/3 cup oil

Lamb with pilaf
(wedding pilaf)

Wash the meat, cut it into pieces and boil in water with a little salt. When the meat is soft, remove it from the pan with a slotted spoon. Strain the liquid, so that it is clear, and return it to the pan along with the rice. The quantities needed for the traditional Cretan pilaf are cups of liquid to 1 cup of rice. When the rice is cooked (after about 15 minutes) add the lemon juice and bring to the boil again. Turn off the heat, and add the softened stakovoutiro to the pilaf.

In many parts of Crete a chicken is boiled together with the lamb, in order to enrich the broth. The cooking method is the same.

1 kg lamb, from a larger (two-year old) animal

½ kg rice

Juice of two lemons

3-4 tbs stakovoutiro (thick, butter-like cream)

Salt

Lamb with potatoes in oven

Wash the meat and cut it into portions. If you have a leg of lamb, leave it whole, making a few cuts into it so that it will roast better. Brush with oil and place in a baking dish. Now peel the potatoes, which should preferably be small ones so that they can be left whole. If they are large, however, cut them into moderately sized pieces and make some slits in them. Put them in the dish around the meat, add the salt and pepper, thyme, lemon juice and the remaining oil and roast in a moderate oven for about 2 hours.

1 kg lamb

½ kg potatoes

Juice of 1 lemon

Thyme

Salt, pepper

½ cup olive oil

'Mayierítsa'

Wash the intestines well and blanch them in boiling water for ten minutes. Drain, allow to cool, and then chop them finely. Heat the oil in a pan and sauté the onion, finely chopped. Add the spring onions, also finely chopped, and the intestines. Stir constantly for about 10 minutes and then add the coarsely chopped lettuce, dill, salt and pepper. Add water (or stock) and leave to cook over a low heat. After 20 minutes, add the rice and leave to cook for a further 15 minutes. Prepare the egg-and-lemon as follows: Beat the egg yolks and slowly add the lemon juice, then take 1 tbs of the liquid from the pan and add it gradually to the egg and lemon mixture. Pour this into the pan, shake it well to distribute evenly, turn off the heat and leave the mixture to bubble a couple of times. 'Mayierítsa' is served hot and constitutes the traditional dish eaten at Easter on the night of the Resurrection.

1 kg lambs' offal
(liver, heart,
intestines)
1 onion
5 spring onions
5 tbs rice
1 lettuce
½ cup finely
chopped dill
5 tbs olive oil

2 lemons
2 egg yolks
1 tsp flour
Salt, pepper

Gioúlbasi'

Cut the meats into cubes, wash them, drain well and place them in a bowl. Add the onions, garlic, peppers, salt, pepper, and cumin and mix well. Finally, add the cheese and the butter, incorporating them thoroughly in the mixture. Transfer the meat to the greaseproof paper sheets and tie them up securely into parcels with string. For greater security, wrap each one again in another sheet and tie as before. Place in the oven and bake at 180-200 C for about 1 ½ hours.

1 ½ kg various types of meat, without bones (beef, lamb, pork)

2 green peppers

3 cloves garlic, finely chopped

3 onions

½ kg kefalograviera cheese

½ cup butter

Large quantity of pepper

Small amount of cumin

Salt

3-4 sheets of greaseproof paper

String

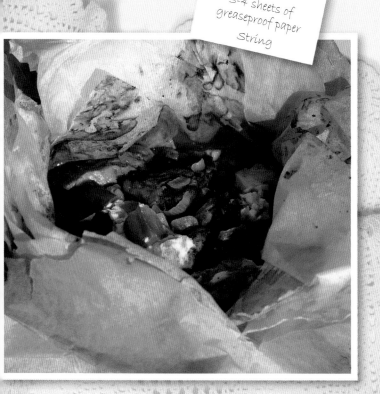

'Spetsofài', from Pelion

Wash the peppers, remove the seeds and cut them into large pieces. Prepare the tomatoes in the same way. Cut the sausages into small pieces or rounds and fry them in a little of the olive oil. Remove from the frying pan, drain them and put them in a baking dish. Similarly, fry the peppers and add them to the dish with the sausages. To the same frying pan, add the chopped tomatoes with the finely chopped garlic, bay leaf, salt, pepper and wine. When these ingredients have boiled a couple of times to form a sauce, add it to the dish with the sausages and peppers. Scatter over the finely chopped parsley, mix together, pour in the remaining oil and leave to boil until the sauce has thickened.

1 kg country sausages

1 kg green peppe

3-4 ripe tomatoe

3-4 cloves of garlic

½ bunch of parsley

1 ½ cups olive oil

½ cup red wine

Bay leaf

Salt, pepper

Pork with leeks

Cut the pork into medium-sized pieces, wash and leave it to drain. Put the oil into a pan and sauté the finely chopped onion with the meat. As soon as it brown, quench' it with the wine, add 1-2 cups of water and leave to cook over a low heat. Shortly before it is completely cooked, add the leeks, which have been washed and cut into medium-sized pieces. Season and leave to cook until a thickish sauce remains with the meat.

1 kg pork
1 kg leeks
1 onion
1/2 cup oil
1/2 cup white wine
Salt, pepper

Pork with celery

Cut the meat into portions, season and place in a pan with water to boil. When it has partly cooked, add the oil, finely chopped onion and the celery, which has been washed and cut into pieces about 5 cms in length. Leave to simmer for about 1 hour.

1 kg pork
1 1/2 kg celery
2-3 onions
2 lemons
Salt, pepper
1 cup olive oil

Smoked pork

Cut the pork into elongated strips and wash them well. Place them in a container full of vinegar and leave them for 2-3 days. Then season well and hang them about half a metre directly above the place where you are going to light the fire. Try to make the fire from twigs of sage, bay or another Cretan aromatic plant, so that the meat will absorb their aroma and be even more delicious. Cover the fire with ash so that it smokes constantly, and leave the meat hanging over it, to cook and brown in the smoke. This is an excellent appetizer to serve with wine and can be kept for a number of days.

Lean pork, without fat

Vinegar

Salt, pepper

Pork with chickpeas

The evening before you intend to make the dish, place the chickpeas in a bowl of water and leave them overnight to soften.

Cut the meat into small portions, wash it and leave it to drain. Heat the oil in a pan and then sauté the meat and the finely chopped onion together until they brown. Add the tomatoes, also finely chopped, salt, pepper and a little water, and leave the meat to simmer for 10 minutes. Now add the chickpeas and enough water to cover, and leave the dish to simmer until the meat is well done and is left with its sauce.

1 kg pork
1 onion
4-5 ripe tomatoes
1/2 kg chickpeas
1 cup oil
Salt, pepper

Pork with sun-dried tomatoes, in a pot

Boil the meat for about 10 minutes and then place it in a pot. Add the onion, cut into slices, the tomatoes cut into cubes, the peppers cut into rounds, and the sun-dried tomatoes. Season, add the allspice, oil and 1 cup of water, and cover the pot. Place in a moderate oven for about 2 hours. Check during the cooking time to see if additional water is needed. Just before the cooking is completed, add the finely chopped parsley.

1 kg pork
1 onion
2 tomatoes
1 green pepper
5-6 sun-dried tomatoes
½ cup olive oil
A little parsley
Salt, pepper, allspice

Brawn made from a pig's head

Wash the head, leave for a few hours and wash it again. Boil it in a large amount of water, initially removing the scum with a slotted spoon, and then add the carrots and seasonings. Cover the pan and leave the head to simmer for several hours. When it is ready, strain it and place it on a plate. Strain the liquid through a sieve and return it to the pan. Cut the carrots into little pieces and place them in moulds. Do the same with the eggs, arranging them in patterns on the base of the moulds so that the brawn will have a nice pattern on the surface when it is turned out of the mould. Meanwhile cut up the lean meat from the head into small pieces and put them to boil once again in the liquid. Turn off the heat and add the lemon juice. Finally, with a spoon, add the liquid and pieces of meat to the moulds containing the carrots and eggs, taking care not to dislodge them. Leave the liquid to cool and then transfer the moulds to the refrigerator. When the brawn has finally set, turn it out from the moulds to serve.

1 medium-sized pig's head

2-3 hard-boiled eggs

4 carrots

Salt, pepper

Lemon juice

Browned pork

Wash the meat, cut it into pieces and season. Pour the oil into the pan and when it is hot add the meat, taking care that all the pieces touch the bottom of the pan. Turn the pieces frequently until they are browned. Reduce the heat, add the rosemary, cover the pan and leave the meat to cook in the oil and its own juices until it is tender.

1½ kg pork
½ cup oil
Rosemary
Salt

Youvarlakia
(boiled meat balls)

Put the minced beef, onion, rice, parsley and one cup of water into a bowl and mix well, finally adding the meringue. Form the mixture into little balls and roll them in flour. Bring 2 litres of water to the boil and then add a little salt, oil, and the meat balls. Leave to cook for about 1 ½ hours. When they are ready, beat the egg yolks and without stopping, add the lemon juice and a little of the liquid from the pan. Add this mixture to the pan and shake to distribute it evenly. Turn off the heat and serve immediately.

1 kg minced beef
1 coffee cup of rice
2 chopped onions
3 tbs flour
3 egg yolks
1 egg white beaten to a meringue
Juice of 2 lemons
1 bunch of finely chopped parsley
Salt, pepper
1 cup oil

Soutzoukakia (spicy meat rissoles)

Mix the meat in a bowl with the stale bread (which you have first soaked in the wine), the pounded garlic, egg, salt, pepper and cumin. When the ingredients are well mixed, form spherical or elongated soutzoukakia and leave them to rest for about an hour. Then heat the oil to a very high temperature in a pan and lightly fry the soutzoukakia. Add the chopped tomatoes, 1 cup of water, and a little salt, and as soon as the sauce begins to thicken transfer both soutzoukakia and sauce to a baking dish. Cook in the oven for around half an hour.

½ kg minced meat
2 slices of stale bread
4-5 ripe tomatoes
2 cloves of garlic
1 egg
½ cup red wine
½ tsp cumin
Salt, pepper
½ cup oil

Minced beef with macaroni

Heat the oil in a pan and add the minced meat. Stir for a few minutes, add the finely chopped onion and sauté all together. Pour over the wine and add the finely chopped tomatoes. Season, and if necessary add a little water. Cover the pan and leave the meat to cook over a moderate heat, until it is tender in the sauce.

Meanwhile, boil the macaroni in a large quantity of salted water. Drain, and if liked, 'singe' with a little oil (heat a little oil to a high temperature in a pan, turn off the heat and add the macaroni, stirring so that it is all coated with the oil). Serve the macaroni on a plate with the meat sauce poured over it.

½ kg minced beef
1 onion
2-3 ripe tomatoes
½ glass of red wine
½ kg macaroni
(use spaghetti)
½ cup oil
Salt, pepper

'Pastítsio

½ kg thick macaroni

1 kg minced meat
½ cup olive oil
1 onion
½ cup red wine
3 ripe tomatoes
1 cinnamon stick
½ cup grated kefalotyri cheese

For the béchamel:
3 tbs butter
7 tbs flour or cornflour
3 cups milk
Nutmeg
Salt, pepper
½ cup grated kefalotyri cheese
Breadcrumbs

2 egg yolks

Macaroni: This should be boiled in salted water, then strained and rinsed with cold water to prevent it from sticking together and left to one side (optional: add a tbs of butter or a little oil to the pan and as soon as it is hot, 'sear' the macaroni in it.

Minced meat: Put the oil in the pan and when it is very hot, immediately sauté the minced meat with the finely chopped onion. 'Quench' with the wine and then add the chopped tomatoes, salt, pepper, cinnamon stick and 1 cup of water. Allow the meat to boil gently until it is left with its sauce, if necessary adding a little more water. When it is ready, remove the pan from the heat and add ½ cup of grated kefalotyri cheese. Mix well together.

Béchamél: Put the butter into a saucepan and as soon as it has melted, add the flour. Mix well together with a wooden spoon until the flour has dissolved completely. Lower the heat, and without ceasing to stir the mixture, slowly add the milk which has previously been warmed slightly. When the mixture thickens, remove it from the heat and add the salt, pepper and nutmeg. Leave it to cool and then add the beaten egg yolk.

Distribute half of the macaroni in a buttered baking dish. Spread the minced meat on top, and then add the rest of the macaroni. Finally, pour over the béchamel, then scatter over the cheese and the breadcrumbs. Bake the pastítsio in moderate oven for about ¾ hour, until the surface has browned.

Aubergine 'little shoes'

½ kg beef mince

11 elongated aubergines

2 finely chopped onions

1 bunch finely chopped parsley

3 finely chopped tomatoes

Cinnamon

Salt, pepper

1 cup oil

Wash the aubergines, cut away a long slice along their length and scoop out the flesh with a spoon, so that they resemble 'boats'. The stem can be left on. Fry them lightly and allow them to drain until you proceed to prepare the meat. Put ½ cup of oil into a pan, bring it to a high heat and sauté the onions. Add the meat and stir together. Add the tomatoes, parsely, cinnamon, salt and pepper and allow to cook for about half and hour. Put the aubergines into a baking dish, fill them with the meat mixture and if liked, add a layer of béchamel on top. Bake for about 30 minutes.

Cabbage 'dolmades' with egg and lemon

Set a saucepan of water to boil. Meanwhile, remove the outer leaves from the cabbage (retain them for later use) and cut into the base of the stalk deeply and in a circular motion, until you reach the centre of the cabbage. Place it in the water with the base of the stalk downwards and leave it to cook until it softens. Remove from the heat, drain it well and when it is cold, separate off the leaves. If the cabbage is large, cut it into two, removing the thick parts.

For the filling: finely chop the onion and sauté it in the oil. Add the meat, seasonings, oregano and a little water and allow all to boil once or twice. Now add the rice, stir the mixture well and allow it to come to the boil again. When the filling is ready, spread the outer leaves of the cabbage which you have retained over the base of a pan. Now place 1 tbs of the filling on each leaf, roll it up, and arrange the rolls on the cabbage leaves in the pan. If there are a lot of rolls, arrange them in two layers. Spread leaves over the second layer again. Add one glass of water and cover the dolmades with a plate, so that they remain immobile and do not come apart. Place the pan on a medium heat and cook for about ¾ hour.

Make the sauce as follows: melt the butter,

1 white cabba[ge]
½ kg pork mi[nce]
1 cup rice for filling
1 onion
2-3 cloves of gar[lic]
1 cup oil
Salt, pepper, oregano

Sauce:
2 eggs
Juice of 2 lemons
2 tbs butter
2 tbs flour

dd the flour and stir well together until slightly browned. Remove he pan from the heat and add a little of the juices from the lolmades, stirring constantly to avoid lumps. Beat the eggs and gradually add the lemon. Mix the butter mixture with the lemon and return the sauce to a low heat, taking care that it does not boil. When the dolmades are ready, remove the large cabbage leaves from the top of the pan, and serve the dolmades on a plate with the sauce poured over them.

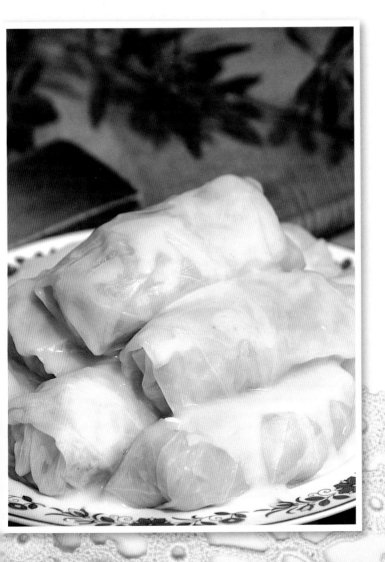

Meat rissoles with potatoes in the oven

Peel and wash the potatoes, then cut them into medium-sized pieces. Season with salt and spread them out in a baking dish. Make the rissoles: mix the meat in a large bowl with the bread, egg, finely chopped onion, salt and pepper. Form into medium-sized balls and place them on top of the potatoes. At the same time, make the sauce: heat the oil in a pan and sauté the finely chopped onion. Add the tomatoes, also finely chopped, salt, pepper, sugar, thyme and one cup of water. Allow the sauce to simmer for about 10 minutes. Pour over the meat rissoles and place the dish in the oven for about 1 hour.

1 kg minced meat (pork and beef mixed)
3 slices of bread, soaked in water and squeezed well
1 egg
1 onion
Salt, pepper
4-5 medium-sized potatoes

For the sauce:
3-4 ripe tomatoes
1 onion
1 tsp sugar
Salt, pepper, thyme
½ cup oil

Moussaka

Cut the vegetables into slices and fry each type separately. Heat the oil and sauté the onion with the meat. Add the chopped tomatoes, parsley, salt and pepper and leave to simmer for about 20 minutes. Spread a layer of fried potatoes in a dish, put a layer of courgettes on top, and then the meat mixture and the aubergines. Finally, pour over a layer of béchamel and put the dish into a preheated oven for about 45 minutes.

700 gr minced beef

2 large aubergines

1 kg potatoes

4-5 courgettes

2 tomatoes

1 onion

Parsley

Salt, pepper

½ cup oil and extra oil for frying

Béchamel (see 'sauces')

1/2 kg minced meat

4 slices of bread, soaked in water, or 100 gr breadcrumbs

1 finely chopped onion

1 egg

3 tbs oil

Vinegar

Salt, pepper, oregano

1 cup flour

Oil for frying

Keftedakia

Mix together all the ingredients (apart from the flour) in a bowl to a homogeneous mass. Form into balls, roll them in flour and fry in very hot oil, turning them constantly so that they do not burn and are cooked from all sides.

Stuffed courgettes with egg and lemon

Wash the courgettes, remove a little from the top and bottom and then remove the flesh with a teaspoon or a corer (retain 1 cup of the flesh for use in the recipe). Salt the inside surfaces, cover them, and then prepare the filling: Heat a little oil to a high temperature and sauté the meat with the onion. Turn off the heat and add the rice, finely chopped parsley, 1 cup of the flesh from the courgettes, salt and pepper. Stir well together and fill the courgettes with the mixture. Do not overfill, as the rice will swell. Place them in a pan either slightly tilted on their sides or standing upright, and add the oil, 2 cups of water, salt and pepper. Cover the pan, turn the heat to low, and cook for about 1 ½ hours, adding more water if necessary, so that a good amount of sauce is formed. When the food is ready, prepare the egg and lemon as follows: beat the eggs and without stopping, add the lemon juice and a little of the sauce from the pan. Pour it over the courgettes, shaking the pan to distribute it evenly, and turn off the heat.

1.5 kg courgettes
½ kg minced beef
½ kg long-grain rice
1 onion
½ bunch parsley
1 cup oil
Salt, pepper

Egg and lemon sauce

2 egg yolks
2 lemons

Snails in the frying pan ('bourbouristi')

Place the snails in a bowl with water to soften and then with a little knife remove the impurities from their shells. Place a frying pan on the heat and cover the base of it with salt. Scatter the snails over the salt with the shells upwards and leave for a while. Now add the oil and a few minutes later, the vinegar and rosemary. Cover the pan and when the contents come to the boil, reduce the heat.

½ kg snails
1 cup vinegar
1 sprig of rosemary
Salt
½ cup oil

SEAFOOD
&
FISH

Cuttlefish in wine sauce

Remove the hard parts and the ink from the cuttlefish and cut them into medium-sized pieces. Pour the oil into a pan and sauté the onions, finely chopped, with the cuttlefish. As soon as they brown, pour over the wine and add the finely chopped tomatoes and tomato paste. Season and add the bay leaf. Stir well, lower the heat, cover the pan and leave to cook until the cuttlefish are tender and left only with their sauce.

1 kg cuttlefish

3 medium-sized onions

1 cup white wine

1 cup oil

3 ripe tomatoes

1 cup tomato paste

1 bay leaf

Salt, pepper

Cuttlefish with spinach

Remove the hard parts and the ink from the cuttlefish (if liked, retain a little ink and put it into a bowl of water) and cut them into pieces. Pour the oil into a pan and sauté the finely chopped onion, fennel, dill, mint and finally, the cuttlefish. Pour over the wine and add a little of the water into which you put the ink, taking care not to stir up the water because this will cause the sand to swirl up and mix with it. Reduce the heat and leave the cuttlefish to cook until tender. Meanwhile, wash and finely chop the spinach. When the cuttlefish are partly cooked, add the spinach to the pan, season, mix well and allow it to cook with the cuttlefish over a low heat for about another 15-20 minutes.

1 kg cuttlefish
1½ kg spinach
1 cup oil
3 onions
1 bunch of fennel
1 bunch of dill
A few mint leaves
1 cup white wine
Salt, pepper

Stuffed cuttlefish

Prepare the cuttlefish, removing the hard parts and the ink. Wash them and leave to drain. Prepare, wash and chop the spinach into large pieces. Sauté for 5 minutes in half of the oil with 1 finely chopped onion. Now stuff the cuttlefish with the spinach. Close them carefully and place them in a pan with the remaining oil and chopped onions. Sauté for a few minutes and then 'quench' with the wine. A few minutes later, add the chopped tomatoes, finely chopped fennel, seasonings and a little water. Leave to cook over a low heat until the cuttlefish are tender.

1 kg cuttlefish

1½ kg spinach

1 bunch of fennel

3 onions

1 cup oil

3 ripe tomatoes

1 cup red wine

Salt, pepper

Cuttlefish with their ink

1 kg cuttlefish

1 cup oil

2 onions

1/2 cup white wine

Salt, pepper

Remove the hard parts and the ink from the cuttlefish. Retain the ink from about 3-4 cuttlefish and place it in a bowl with water, so that the sand in the ink sinks to the bottom. Wash the cuttlefish and cut into pieces. Heat the oil to a high temperature in a pan and sauté the finely chopped onions and cuttlefish pieces until they are lightly browned. Pour over the wine, add 1 cup of water with the ink from the bowl, and then another cup of water. Stir well, cover the pan, lower the heat and cook for about half and hour, until the cuttlefish are tender and left with only a thickish sauce.

Fried salted, dried cod

Place the cod in a good amount of water to remove the salt and leave overnight. Next day, wash it well, prepare it and cut into portions. Beat together the flour, salt, beaten egg and a little water to make a batter, dip the cod pieces in it and then fry them in very hot olive oil.

This dish goes very well with skordalia (see sauces).

½ kg salted, dried cod

1 egg

1 cup flour

Olive oil for frying

Cuttlefish in wine sauce

Remove the hard parts and the ink from the cuttlefish and cut them into medium-sized pieces. Pour the oil into a pan and sauté the onions, finely chopped, with the cuttlefish. As soon as they brown, pour over the wine and add the finely chopped tomatoes and tomato paste. Season and add the bay leaf. Stir well, lower the heat, cover the pan and leave to cook until the cuttlefish are tender and left only with their sauce.

1 kg cuttlefish
3 medium-sized onions
1 cup white wine
1 cup oil
3 ripe tomatoes
1 cup tomato paste
1 bay leaf
Salt, pepper

Stuffed squid

Remove the hard parts, ink and eyes of the squid. Pull off the tentacles and chop them. Wash the squid well, removing the dark membrane and leaving only the white flesh. Put half of the oil into a pan and sauté the finely chopped onions. Add the tentacles, stir well together and add the finely chopped dill, seasonings and 1 cup of water. Lower the heat and after about a quarter of an hour add the rice and two cups of water. As soon as the rice is cooked, turn off the heat, add the lemon juice and leave the mixture to cool. Fill the squid using a teaspoon, taking care to leave a space for the rice to swell. Close the squid with toothpicks and place them in a baking dish, close to each other. Pour over the remaining oil and ½ cup of water, season well, cover the dish for the first part of the cooking time with aluminium foil, and bake in the oven for about half and hour.

1 kg medium-sized squid
1 cup oil
1 cup rice
2 onions
1 bunch of dill
salt, pepper
1 lemon

Fried squid

1 kg squid

Flour

2 lemons

Salt

Olive oil for frying

Prepare and wash the squid. Mix the flour with the salt, roll the squid in the mixture and fry them in very hot oil, turning constantly. When they are ready, remove them from the pan with a slotted spoon and place them on kitchen paper on a plate, to drain. Serve hot garnished with lemon slices.

If liked, the squid can also be cooked on the top of the stove in a pan; in that case, add the oil, enough water to cover, the juice of another lemon and season well. Cover the pan and leave to cook until the squid are tender and most of the liquid has been absorbed. To serve, the small amount of sauce that remains can be bound with a little corn flour and poured over the squid.

Prawn 'saganáki'

Pour the oil into a pan and add the
chopped tomatoes, salt and pepper.
Leave this sauce to cook and when
it thickens, add the prawns. If
necessary, add a little water and
cook for about 10 more minutes,
until the prawns are done. Finally,
add the feta cheese and leave the
pan on the heat for a few minutes,
until the cheese has melted. Scatter
over the oregano, and serve hot.

½ kg prawns,
shelled

250 gr feta cheese

3 tomatoes

1 cup olive oil

Oregano

Salt, pepper

Octopus with short macaroni shells

1 kg octopus

1/2 kg short macaroni shells

3-4 ripe tomatoes

1 large onion

1/2 cup red wine

Salt, pepper

1 cup olive oil

Place the octopus in water the night before you intend to cook it, for it to tenderize. If it is already soft, cut it into pieces, wash them and leave to strain. Heat the oil in a pan and sauté the finely chopped onion. Add the octopus, stir well and 'quench' with the wine. Add water and leave to cook over a low heat. When it is partly cooked, add the finely chopped tomatoes, salt, and pepper and leave to cook well. Remove the octopus from the pan with a slotted spoon and cook the macaroni in the sauce that has remained, adding water if necessary. Mix together the octopus and the macaroni and serve hot.

Octopus in wine

Wash the octopus well. Remove the beak, eyes, and the ink from the stomach sac. Cut the octopus into small pieces and place in a pan over a low heat for about half an hour, without water, to cook in their own moisture; cover the pan. When the octopus is soft, strain off the water and retain it for later use; add the oil and finely chopped onion. As soon as the contents of the pan come to the boil, 'quench' them with the wine and then add the chopped tomatoes and bay leaves. Cover the pan and leave to cook over a low heat until the octopus is really tender and the sauce has thickened. If necessary, add a little of the retained liquid or some more wine. Do not add water, otherwise the octopus will toughen.

1 kg octopus
1 small onion
1/2 cup oil
1 cup wine
3-4 tomatoes
1-2 bay leaves
Pepper

Octopus in vinegar

Wash the octopus and boil it in enough water to cover with the finely chopped onions. When it is tender, remove it from the heat and cut into small pieces. Place them in a bowl and add the oil, vinegar, oregano, salt and pepper. Keep covered in the refrigerator and serve cold as an appetizer.

2 kg octopus
2 onions
½ cup oil
Vinegar
Oregano
Salt, pepper

Octopus with potatoes

Wash the octopus and boil it in enough water to cover, until it has softened. Strain and cut the octopus into pieces; retain the cooking liquid for later use. Finely chop the onion and sauté it in very hot oil. Add the chopped tomatoes, finely chopped garlic, bay leaf, potatoes cut into large pieces, octopus, and the liquid. If needed, add a little more water. Season well and cook until a thick sauce is left.

1 kg octopus
1 kg potatoes
4 tomatoes
3 onions
3 cloves of garlic
1 cup oil
1 bay leaf
Salt, pepper

Pilaf of mussels

Place the mussels in a bowl with a large amount of water and leave for two hours. Scrape their shells with a knife, wash them and boil them in a little water for a few minutes until they open. Retain those that open and strain off the liquid with a very fine sieve. In another pan, sauté the finely chopped onion and add the rice. Stir the mixture a couple of times, throw in the mussels and add the retained liquid. Season with salt and pepper, and leave to boil until the rice is cooked.

1 kg mussels
3 onions
2 cups rice
A little olive oil
Salt, pepper

'Liókafta', from Mytilene

Clean the fish and make an opening in one side of each. Remove the central bone and dust the inside of the fish with the oil, oregano, salt and pepper. Close with a toothpick and hang them up on a string, taking care that they remain horizontal and that insects and flies do not come near them. One day later, roast them over the charcoals or on the grill. Add lemon, and the 'mezés' is ready.

Medium-sized fish
(bogue, mackerel etc)
Oregano
Salt, pepper
Olive oil, lemon

Boiled fish and fish soup

Prepare and wash the fish and the vegetables. Cut the carrots, celery, potatoes and onion into medium-sized pieces and leave the courgettes whole. Half-fill a saucepan with water and add the oil, carrots, onions and celery. Boil for about 15 minutes and then add the potatoes, courgettes, fish and seasonings. After about half an hour, when the fish and vegetables have cooked, remove them from the pan with a slotted spoon and transfer to a plate. If liked, retain about half of the vegetables and one piece of the fish, pulp them through a sieve and add them to the liquid in the pan. Bring to the boil and add the rice. Leave to cook for 20 minutes until soft and then turn off the heat. Make the egg and lemon mixture: Beat the yolks of the eggs and without stopping

2 kg fish
(grouper, bass,
cod, rascasse etc)

1/2 kg courgettes

1/2 kg carrots

3 potatoes

2 onions

1/2 cup oil

1 bunch of celery

1/2 cup rice

salt, pepper

2 egg yolks

2 lemons

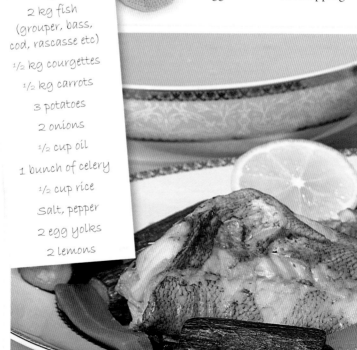

'Bourdéto', from the Ionian islands

1 kg fish
(rascasse, sea
bream, mullet)
1 cup olive oil
½ kg onions
2 cloves of garlic
1 tbs hot paprika
½ kg potatoes
2 tbs tomato
paste
Salt

Put the oil in a pan and sauté the finely chopped onions. Add the garlic, also finely chopped, the tomato paste, salt and paprika. Leave the sauce to simmer gently for about half an hour. Meanwhile, wash and prepare the fish. Add them to the pan along with the potatoes, which have been cut into medium-sized chunks. Leave to cook over a low heat for about half an hour.

gradually add the lemon juice and a little of the soup. Now pour the mixture into the pan, stir well, and the soup is ready.

Anchovies with oregano

Prepare and clean the anchovies, discarding the heads. Rinse well. Place them in a dish, dust with oregano, sprinkle over the lemon juice, season and add a little water, and bake in the oven for about 40 minutes.

1 kg anchovies
2 lemons
1 tsp oregano
Salt, pepper
½ cup olive oil

Fish in the oven

Clean and prepare the fish, wash it and if large, cut it into slices. Season, sprinkle over the lemon juice and leave to one side. Prepare the sauce: Heat the oil in a pan and sauté the finely chopped onions and garlic. Add the finely chopped parsley, organo, and 'quench' with the wine. Add the chopped tomatoes and seasoning, then bring to the boil once or twice to thicken. Spread the fish out in a baking dish and pour over the sauce. Place in the oven and leave to cook at a moderate temperature for about one hour.

1 kg large fish
1 cup oil
2 onions
2 cloves of garlic
½ bunch of parsley
1 glass of white wine
3 tomatoes
Juice of 1 lemon
Salt, pepper, oregano

CONFECTIONERY

Little cheese envelopes with honey

Beat the eggs and add the oil. Mix well together and add 1 cup of water, the baking soda and the flour, to form a moderately stiff dough. Leave aside, wrapped in a teacloth, and prepare the filling: mix together the cheese and eggs, cinnamon and mint. Now roll out the dough into a sheet, using a rolling pin (or a pasta machine). Cut out circles with a glass. Place a teaspoon of the filling on each circle and fold it over to form a closed half-moon shape. Heat some oil to a high temperature and fry the envelopes. Serve hot, with honey.

For the pastry:
1 kg flour
2 eggs
1/2 tsp baking soda
1/3 cup oil

Filling:
1 kg myzithra (cream cheese)
2 eggs
1 tsp cinnamon
A little chopped mint

Honey

Lychnarakia
('little lights')

Prepare the pastry dough by mixing the ingredients together and then set it aside, covered with a cloth. In a bowl, mix the myzithra and the crumbled anthotyro well together with the eggs and mint. Roll out the dough into a sheet. Using a cup or a glass (according to the desired size of the lychnarakia) cut out rounds and place a teaspoon of the cheese filling on each. Close them, forming half-moon shapes. The pastry sheet can also be cut into square pieces, the filling placed on top and then the four sides folded over towards the centre leaving a little of the filling visible. Whatever shape is chosen, place the lychnarakia on an oiled baking sheet and brush them with egg. A little sesame may also be scattered over them. Bake for about an hour in a moderate oven.

Pastry:

½ kg flour

1 cup milk

1 tbs olive oil

As much water as needed

Filling:

½ kg myzithra (cream cheese)

½ kg anthotyro (soft cheese)

4 eggs

1-2 mint leaves

Sarikopites

Put the flour in a bowl and open up a well in the centre. Add the oil, raki and salt. Mix to a dough, adding the water gradually, as much as is required, to form a moderate to firm dough. When it is ready form it into a ball, cover and leave to rest for one hour. Meanwhile, put the cheese into a bowl and mash it with a fork. Roll out the dough into a thin sheet and cut into long strips about 20 x 7 cms. Spread a spoonful of cheese along the whole length, roll it up in the same direction and close the edges well. Now bend the strips into a snail shape to form the sarikopites. Fry them in very hot oil and serve either dusted with cinnamon and sugar or with honey.

Pastry:
½ kg flour
3 tbs oil
2 tbs raki
Salt
1 cup of water

½ kg xinomyzithra (cream cheese)
Honey (or sugar and cinnamon)
Oil for frying

'Bougátsa', from Sérres

Boil the milk together with the semolina, stirring until it has thickened. Meanwhile, mix the sugar, eggs and vanilla and beat well together. Add this mixture to the pan containing the milk, and stir until the ingredients bind and a smooth cream is achieved. Remove the pan from the heat and butter a baking dish. Spread half of the fyllo pastry in the dish, adding the sheets one by one and brushing each with melted butter. Pour in the cream and fold over the lower layers of the fyllo pastry which hang over the sides of the dish. Place the remainder of the pastry on top, brushing each sheet individually with butter. Score the surface, brush it with butter, and bake in a moderate oven for about ¾ hour, until the pastry is lightly browned. Serve the bougátsa with powdered sugar and cinnamon dusted over the surface.

½ kg fyllo pastry
4 cups milk
1 cup sugar
¾ cup semolina
4 eggs
2 sachets of vanilla
1 cup butter
Powdered sugar
Cinnamon

'Barboulé', from Kefalonía

Put the almonds and the sugar in a pan and turn on the heat. After the sugar has melted, spread out the thick mass thus obtained on a marble surface. Cut into small pieces immediately, and leave to cool.

1 cup of unsalted almonds, roasted and pounded

1 cup sugar

(If desired, greater quantities can be used, but always in the same proportion)

'Mandoláto', from Zákynthos

Boil the sugar with 2-3 tbs of water until it has
dissolved well, and a thick syrup is formed.
Likewise, add the honey to ½ cup of water and
boil to dissolve it. Mix the two syrups (one of
sugar, the other of honey) and stir well together.
Beat the egg whites well, and when a stiff
meringue has formed, add the syrup mixture.
Return the pan to the heat and as soon as the
mixture is hot add the almonds, which have
previously been coarsely chopped and toasted.
When the mixture toughens a little, remove the
pan from the heat. Lay out a cloth on a marble
surface and spread the mixture from the pan
on it. Cut it into pieces, leave to cool, and wrap
in paper.

100 gr sugar
500 gr honey
5 egg whites
300 gr almonds

Kataïfi

In a large bowl mix the walnuts, almonds, toast crumbs, sugar, cinnamon powder and clove to form the filling. Put the oil into a little bowl, dip your fingers into it and pull out the pastry strands. By this means, the pastry receives as much oil as it needs, evenly distributed. Now take a little of it, put a spoonful of the filling on it, and roll it up to form a sausage. Repeat until all the filling and pastry has been used, and then place the rolls in a dish close to each other. When the dish is full, sprinkle over a little water. Bake in a moderate oven for about half and hour until the rolls begin to brown. Care is needed, as the pastry burns easily. Remove the dish from the oven, prepare the syrup by mixing all the ingredients in a saucepan and bringing them to the boil a few time until the syrup thickens. When it is ready and still hot, pour it over the rolls, cover them and allow them to cool.

1 kg kataïfi pastry
½ kg chopped walnuts
½ kg chopped almonds
3 pieces of toast, crumbed
½ cup sugar
Cinnamon powder
Ground clove
1 cup oil

Syrup:
6 cups of water
6 cups sugar
2 tbs honey
1 cinnamon stick

Loukoumades (honey puffs) with yeast

Put the yeast into 1 cup of the warm water and stir it well to dissolve it. Put the flour, salt, yeast, honey and the remainder of the water into a bowl and mix well to a batter with a spoon. Cover the mixture and leave in a warm place to rise. When the mixture has almost doubled and there are bubbles on the surface, it is ready. Pour a good amount of olive oil into a pan and bring it to a very high temperature. With your hand, take a small amount of the mixture, clench your fist and with a spoon remove the mixture that oozes out. Toss the content of your hand into the oil and repeat until the pan is full. Allow the loukoumades to brown, remove them with a slotted spoon and place them to drain on absorbent paper. Serve hot, with honey and sesame.

½ kg flour

1 tbs salt

1 level tbs honey

2 ½ cups of water

½ envelope yeast

Oil for frying

To serve:

Honey

Sesame

'Ekmék kataïfi'

Prepare the cream as follows: mix together the sugar and the eggs. Add the flour, then slowly add the milk. Place the saucepan on the heat and stirring constantly with a wooden spoon, allow the mixture to thicken. Now remove the pan from the heat and add the vanilla and the butter, beating until the latter has dissolved. The cream is ready, and should now be left to cool.
Pull out the kataïfi, 'unravelling' it with your hands, and spread it in a buttered baking dish. Bake in the oven until it has browned. Meanwhile, prepare the syrup by boiling the sugar and water in a saucepan with the flavourings (cinnamon, clove, lemon peel). When it has thickened slightly, remove the spices and lemon peel and pour it over the kataïfi as soon as it is taken out of the oven. Spread the cream on top, and leave in the refrigerator to cool. When it is served, decorate with whipped cream and scatter over the chopped pistachios.

200 gr kataïfi pastry

Syrup:
3/4 cup sugar
2/3 cup water
1 cinnamon stick
2-3 cloves
Lemon peel

Cream:
1 1/2 cups sugar
2 eggs
1 cup flour
2 1/2 cups milk
1 sachet of vanilla
1 cup butter

1/2 kg whipped cream

A few pistachios (from Aegina)

'Baklavás,' from Ioánnina

Place the almonds in boiling water to blanch them and enable their skins to be removed. Dry them, and then chop them and toast in a frying pan. Chop the walnuts. Mix together the almonds, walnuts, sugar, breadcrumbs, cinnamon and clove. Melt the butter and brush a baking dish with it. Spread up to ten sheets of fyllo pastry, each brushed with butter, in the dish, and scatter over some filling. Continue to add alternately individual buttered sheets of fyllo and layers of filling, until about ten sheets of pastry are left. Place these, also individually buttered, on top. Butter the surface of the final sheet, score diagonally to form diamonds and bake in a moderate oven for about 1 – 1 ½ hours, until the top sheet of fyllo pastry has browned. When the baklavás has cooled, pour over the syrup, which is made as follows: boil the sugar in a saucepan with the water. As soon as it has dissolved and the syrup begins to thicken slightly, add the honey and stir together well. Pour the hot syrup over the cold baklavás.

1 ½ kg fyllo pastry for baklavas
300 gr almonds
300 gr walnuts
300 gr butter
2 tbs sugar
3 tbs breadcrumbs
1 tbs cinnamon
1 tsp ground clove

Syrup:
4 cups sugar
4 cups water
½ cup honey
1 cinnamon stick

Tzevremedakia

Begin by making the syrup, since this must be quite cold when we remove the tzevremedakia from the oven. Put the water, sugar and orange slices into a pan and boil them until a syrup is formed. This should be quite thin - certainly thinner than the syrup used in 'spoon sweets'. Remove the syrup from the heat and leave to cool completely.

1 small whole myzithra
1 egg
½ tsp cinnamon (optional)
½ kg fyllo pastry

Syrup:
4 cups sugar
4 cups of water
1 orange cut into slices

Make the filling by mashing the myzithra and mixing it with the egg and cinnamon (optional). Fold the fyllo pastry in half and cut it into two. Fold it in half again and cut it, thus forming pieces measuring about 20 x 22 cms.

For each tzevremedaki, take two of the sheets of fyllo, oil them and place them on top of each other.

Along the length of the bottom spread a spoonful of the filling and in order to retain it fold over the two sides. Brush the inside of the tzevremedaki with oil and roll up the filling to form a cylinder. Place the rolls in a lightly oiled dish, not too close together, and brush their surfaces with oil. Preheat the oven to 180 C. Put in the dish and lower the heat to 160 C. After half and hour, raise the heat again to 180 C, in order to brown the pastry. As soon as the tzevremedakia are ready, remove them from the oven and pour over the cold syrup.

Poura (walnut rolls)

Prepare the syrup, so that it will be cold when the poura are cooked: boil the water with the sugar and orange slices until a syrup is formed, but not as thick as that for poura. Mix together the chopped walnuts, sugar, breadcrumbs, cinnamon and sesame.

Cut the fyllo pastry exactly as for tzevremedakia, take two of them, brush with oil on the inside and spread the filling over the whole surface (i.e. not as in tzevremedakia, where it is only spread along one side).

Fold over the sides so that the filling cannot escape, brush the inside with oil and roll up into a cylinder. Arrange in a lightly oiled dish, not too close together, and brush the surfaces with oil.

Bake in a preheated oven, exactly as for tzevremedakia. As soon as they are ready, remove from the oven and pour over the cold syrup.

½ kg fyllo pastry

½ kg chopped walnuts

2 tbs sugar

2 tbs breadcrumbs

1 tsp cinnamon

4 tbs sesame

Syrup:

4 cups sugar

4 cups of water

1 orange cut into slices

Galaktoboureko

Butter a baking dish and spread out half of the fyllo pastry in it, buttering each sheet as you lay it on top of the other. Butter the remaining sheets in the same way and set them aside. If using fresh milk, boil it and then allow it to cool. Beat the eggs in your mixer with the extra yolks and sugar. Transfer the mixture to a saucepan and gradually add the milk and semolina. Simmer gently until the mixture thickens. Remove from the heat and add any remaining butter. Pour the filling into the dish, over the fyllo pastry, and cover with the remaining buttered sheets. Score the pastry, so that the galatoboureko will cut easily into portions when cooked. Bake in the oven at 190 C for about 15 minutes and then reduce to 160 C and bake for a further 35 minutes. Meanwhile, make the syrup by boiling the water, sugar and lemon zest together. When you remove the galatoboureko from the oven, immediately pour the syrup (which should have cooled) over it.

300 gr fyllo pastry
½ cup butter
4 cups milk
½ cup sugar
2 eggs + 2 yolks
5 tbs fine semolina
Vanilla

Syrup:
2 cups sugar
1 cup water
Lemon zest

Cake made with olive oil

Put the oil into a bowl with the sugar
and beat very well together. Gradually
add the eggs, milk, vanilla, and lemon
zest and juice. Stir all well together then
slowly add the flour, into which you have
mixed the baking powder.
Oil the bottom of a cake tin and pour in
the mixture. Bake the cake in a preheated
oven for about 45 minutes. If liked, when
the cake is removed from the tin it can be
dusted with powdered sugar.

4 ½ cups flour
1 cup sugar
1½ cups milk
2 eggs
1 tsp baking
powder
Juice and zest of
1 lemon
1 envelope
vanilla
1½ cups oil

Honey pie,
from Sífnos

Fyllo pastry:
250 gr flour
¾ cup butter
¼ cup water
2 tbs powdered sugar

Filling:
500 gr sweet
myzithra cheese
1/3 cup honey
4 eggs
1/3 cup powdered
sugar
1 tbs flour
1 tbs cinnamon

In a bowl, mix together the flour, the
powdered sugar, and the butter and slowly
add water. Mix well to a firm dough.
Form into a ball, cover it and leave it in
the refrigerator for about half an hour.
Meanwhile, prepare the filling as follows:
mash the myzithra, and in a separate bowl
beat the eggs well with the sugar, and then
with the flour. Add the mashed myzithra to
this mixture, along with the honey and 1 tsp of
the cinnamon. Mix all together well.
Roll out the pastry into a sheet, lay it in a
buttered baking dish and trim off the excess
around the edges. Spread the filling on top of it,
and bake in a preheated oven for about one hour.
When the pie has browned, remove it from the
oven and dust the surface with the remaining
cinnamon.

Cake with apples

Beat together the sugar with the oil (or margarine) in your mixer. Add the egg yolks, and then the whites beaten separately to a stiff meringue. Sprinkle the apples with cognac, scatter 2 tbs of sugar over them and add them to the egg mixture with the walnuts.

Finally, mix together the baking powder with the flour and add it slowly. Pour the mixture into an oiled cake tin and bake in a moderate oven for about 1 hour.

½ cup oil
or 150 gr
margarine
1 ½ cups
sugar
2 ½ cups flour
4 eggs
½ envelope of
baking powder
2 ½ cups of
finely chopped
apples
1 cup walnuts
A little cognac

Almond cake

Beat the sugar with the egg yolks until the mixture whitens. Dissolve the baking powder in the cognac and add to the mixture along with the almonds, crumbed rusks, and lemon zest. Beat the egg whites to a stiff meringue and add to the mixture along with the salt. Pour the mixture into a buttered cake tin and bake in a moderate oven for about 45 minutes. Meanwhile, prepare the syrup and pour it over the cake as soon as it is removed from the oven.

3 cups chopped almonds

8 eggs

1 ½ cups sugar

3 rusks, crumbed

2 tsp baking powder

½ small wineglass of cognac

Zest of a lemon

1 pinch of salt

Syrup:

2 cups sugar

1 ½ cups of water

Juice of half a lemon

Almond macaroons

Beat the egg whites well. Add the sugar and continue beating until it is incorporated. Add the finely ground almonds and the lemon zest. Stir well together and form the macaroons like biscuits, placing them on an oiled baking sheet. Bake in a moderate oven for about 20 minutes, until they are browned.

1200 gr ground almonds
600 gr sugar
10 egg whites
Lemon zest

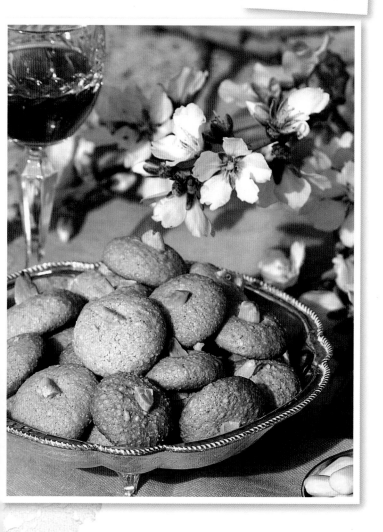

Walnut cake

Beat the oil and the sugar well together, in your mixer. Add the eggs, milk, walnuts, cinnamon, cloves and finally the flour into which you have mixed the baking powder. Pour into an oiled cake tin and bake in a moderate oven for about 45 minutes. When the cake is cooked, allow it to cool and then remove from the tin. Prepare the syrup: Boil the water in a saucepan, add the sugar and then the cognac. Stir well together and leave to boil for about 5 minutes, to form a light syrup. Pour the syrup over the cake while it is still hot.

1 cup olive oil
1 ½ cups sugar
6 eggs
1 cup milk
1 tbs cinnamon
3-4 ground cloves
3 cups chopped walnuts
½ kg flour
2 tsp baking powder

Syrup:
2 cups sugar
2 cups of water
2 tsp cognac

Vasilopita

Cream together the sugar and butter in your mixer. Without stopping the machine, add the egg yolks, milk, almonds (roughly chopped) and the cognac. Dissolve the baking soda in the lemon juice and add to the mixture along with the vanilla. Add the flour mixed with the baking powder. Finally, beat the egg whites in a separate bowl to a stiff meringue and add to the mixture, lightly incorporating them with a spoon, so that the meringue does not 'deflate'. Pour the mixture into a buttered tin and bake in a moderate oven for about 1 hour.

1 cup sugar
1 cup butter
7 eggs
1 cup milk
150 gr almonds
½ cup cognac
1 tsp baking soda
Juice of ½ lemon
1 tsp vanilla
1 tsp baking powder
3 cups flour

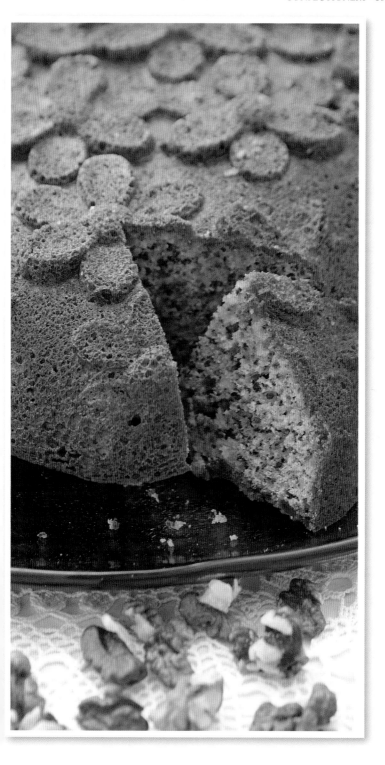

Ravani with coconut

Beat the sugar and oil well together in the mixer and add the eggs one by one; then add the milk and the coconut. Finally, mix together the baking powder with the flour and add it gradually to the mixture, continuing to beat for a while.

Put the mixture into an oiled and lightly floured baking dish or mould and bake in a moderate oven for about one hour. In the meantime, prepare the syrup by boiling the water with the sugar and lemon peel for about five minutes.

When the ravani is ready, remove it from the tin and pour over the syrup.

2/3 cup oil
1 cup sugar
3 eggs
2/3 cups milk
1 1/2 cups coconut
1 1/2 cups flour
1 tsp baking powder

For the syrup:
1 1/2 cups sugar
1 1/2 cups of water
1 tsp lemon juice
Lemon peel

Yogurt cake

1 ½ cups sugar

1 cup butter

2 cups flour

1 ½ cups yogurt

5 eggs

2 tsp baking powder

2 tsp lemon zest

Cream together the butter and sugar and then add the egg yolks and yogurt. Mix together the flour, baking powder and lemon zest and beat the egg whites separately.

Add the flour all in one, with the egg whites, to the yogurt mixture. Stir well together and pour into a buttered tin. Bake in a moderate oven for about 1 hour.

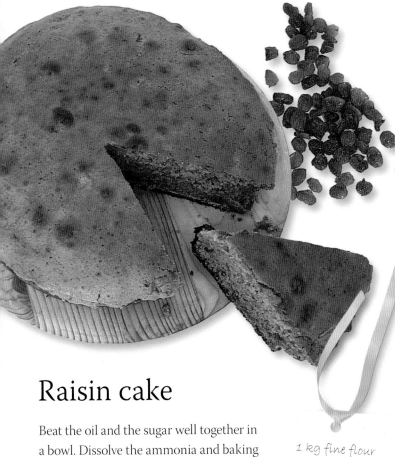

Raisin cake

Beat the oil and the sugar well together in a bowl. Dissolve the ammonia and baking soda in the orange juice and add to the oil and sugar mixture. Add the cinnamon, cloves, lemon zest and raisins. Slowly add the flour, and the mixture is ready.
Pour into an oiled baking tin and bake in a preheated oven for about 1 hour.

1 kg fine flour
½ kg sugar
1 glass of orange juice
1 tsp ground cinnamon
1 tsp baking soda
1 tsp ammonia
Zest of 1 lemon
1 cup of ground raisins
Ground cloves
2 cups oil

Apple cake

Beat the oil and 1 cup of sugar well together, using your mixer. Add the eggs and then, slowly, the flour mixed with the baking powder. The texture will be quite thick and almost crumbly. Puree the apples and mix them with the remaining cup of sugar, cinnamon and walnuts. Take half of the cake mixture and rubbing it through your fingers, spread it over the bottom of a baking dish.

Pour the apple filling on top and then add the rest of the cake mixture in the same way. Bake in a moderate oven for about 30-40 minutes. Dust with powdered sugar when cold.

5 cups flour
2 cups sugar
2 eggs
2 tsp baking powder
1 cup chopped almonds
Cinnamon
6-7 apples
Powdered sugar
1 cup oil

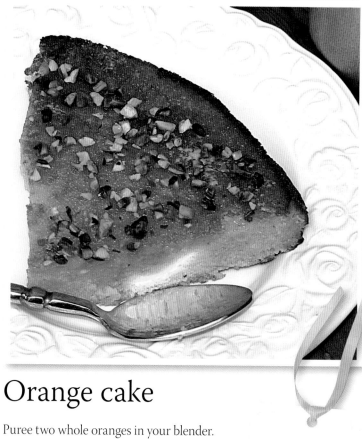

Orange cake

Puree two whole oranges in your blender.
Add the sugar, eggs, milk, semolina, baking
powder and chopped almonds.
Bake the mixture in a moderate oven for 1
¼ hours. Meanwhile prepare the syrup and
pour it over the cake when you take it out of
the oven.

2 oranges
1 cup milk
3 eggs
3 tbs semolina
1 cup sugar
320 gr almonds
1 tsp baking
powder

Syrup:
1 cup sugar
1 cup water
Orange peel

Risogalo
(milk rice pudding)

Put the milk, rice, a little salt and half of the sugar into a saucepan and boil over a low heat until the rice has softened. Meanwhile, beat the egg yolks with the remaining sugar until the mixture is white. When the rice mixture has thickened, remove it from the heat and slowly add the egg mixture, beating continuously. Replace it on the very low heat and beat the mixture until it becomes homogeneous in texture, taking care not to let it boil. Remove from the heat and either serve hot in little bowls, or dust with cinnamon and leave to go cold.

1½ litres milk

1 cup rice

3 egg yolks

6 tbs sugar

Ground cinnamon

Salt

Easter koulourakia

Sieve the flour and mix in the vanilla. Beat the butter with the sugar and add the eggs one by one. Dissolve the ammonia in the milk and add to the mixture along with the flour, all in one. When the mixture is consolidated, knead it with your hands to form an elastic, non-sticky dough. Form sausages about half the thickness of a finger and form them into various shapes, such as snails, plaits, wheels etc. Put them on an oiled baking sheet and brush with beaten egg yolk. Bake in a moderate oven for about 20-25 minutes, until golden brown.

6 eggs
½ kg sugar
1 ½ kg flour
50 gr ammonia
320 gr butter
1 envelope vanilla

Tsoureki made with yeast

Beat the sugar and egg yolks well together, and beat the whites separately. Put the flour into a bowl, make a well in the centre and add the yeast dissolved in a little warm water. Then, slowly add the beaten yolks and sugar, the stiff egg whites and finally the warmed, thinned cream.

Mix well to a dough and leave in a warm place until it has risen. Knead well again and if it sticks to your hands rub them with a little melted butter.

Form the tsourekia into shapes (half-moons, snails, bars) and leave them to rise again. When they are ready, brush them with beaten egg and scatter over the almond slivers. Bake in the oven at 200 C for about half an hour.

1 kg flour
350 gr sugar
½ kg cream
6 eggs
½ tsp ground machlepi
80 gr yeast
½ cup water
A few slivers of almonds

Tsoureki made with sourdough

The evening before you intend to make the tsourekia, mix the sourdough with ½ kg of flour. Leave overnight in a bowl to rise. Next morning, divide the ingredients into two – i.e. 5 eggs, ½ kg sugar, 250 gr cream, 750 gr milk. Beat the egg yolks with half the sugar and the egg whites with the other half. Mix together with the risen sourdough and add as much flour as needed to form a light mixture like that of a cake. Place in a warm spot to rise until it has almost doubled in bulk. Now add the other half of the ingredients to the risen dough, knead and form into tsourekia, in any shape you prefer (plaits, half-moons, snails etc). Place them on a clean cloth and leave in a warm place to rise. When they are ready, put them on an oiled baking dish, brush the surfaces with beaten egg and bake until they are golden brown.

3 kg flour

10 eggs

1 kg sugar

500 gr cream

1½ cups milk

About 1 cup sourdough

Orange koulourakia

Mix the baking powder with the flour and dissolve the baking soda in one small cup of orange juice. Beat the oil together with the sugar in your mixer and when the sugar has dissolved, add 2 eggs. Add the orange juice and dissolved baking soda and, gradually, the flour. When the mixture is thick, remove it from the mixer and knead it with your hands, incorporating the remaining flour. Form little koulouria in whatever shapes you prefer, and place them on an oiled baking sheet. To give them a gloss, brush with beaten egg before putting them in the oven. Bake at a moderate temperature until they are golden brown.

1 cup orange juice
1 cup oil
3 eggs
200 gr sugar
2 tsp baking powder
½ tsp baking soda
1 kg flour

Ladokouloura

Beat the olive oil and the orange juice together and add the sugar, ammonia dissolved in the raki, and one cup of water in which you have boiled the cinnamon. Slowly add the flour and knead to a soft and pliable dough. Form into long sausages with your hands, roll them in the sesame and then cut off pieces 10-12 cms in length; form them into the shape of an S. Place them on an oiled baking dish so that they do not stick, and bake in the oven for about 1 hour, until golden brown.

4 cups fine flour
1 cup orange juice
3 cups sugar
1 tbs ammonia
1 cup raki
1 little stick of cinnamon
2 cups sesame
2 cups olive oil

Melomakarona

Beat the oil well together with the icing sugar. Add the zest and the orange juice into which you have mixed the baking soda, cinnamon, clove, walnuts and milk. Then slowly add the flour mixed with the baking powder to form a soft dough. Now form the melomakarona into circular or elliptical shapes and place them on an oiled baking sheet. Bake in a moderate oven for about 30 minutes.

Meanwhile, make the syrup as follows: Boil the water in a saucepan and add the sugar and honey. When the syrup is ready, and still warm, dunk the melomakarona into it and remove immediately with a slotted spoon.

Arrange them on a plate and scatter over them a mixture of the chopped walnuts, sesame and cinnamon.

6 cups flour
2 cups olive oil
1 cup icing sugar
1 cup milk
1 cup orange juice
1 tsp orange zest
1 tsp cinnamon
1 tsp ground clove
1/2 cup chopped walnuts
1 tsp baking soda
1 tsp baking powder

Syrup:
2 cups water
1 cup honey
1 cup sugar

Kouloura made with grape must

Beat the oil with the sugar well together in your mixer and gradually add the grape must, lye, cognac, cinnamon and clove. Then slowly add the flour and before the dough is formed, add the lemon juice in which you have dissolved the baking soda. Add the remaining flour, but do not allow the mixture to become too stiff. Now form kouloura and place them on an oiled baking tin. Bake at first at 200 C, and then reduce the temperature to 180 and bake until they are a nice golden brown.

1 ½ cups grape must

1 cup oil

1 cup sugar

1 wine glass of lye

½ wine glass of lemon juice

1 tsp baking soda

1 tsp ground cinnamon

1 tsp ground clove

1½ kg flour

Grape must jelly

Sieve the ash, add it to the must and boil together. Leave it to cool and settle for several hours or overnight.

Next day, strain it well and pass it through a very fine sieve. Then take a little of the must and mix it with the flour so as to form a batter. Return the must to the heat and let it boil for 15 minutes. Then add the batter very slowly, beating continuously.

Boil the mixture until it is well thickened. Pour the mixture while hot into bowls or plates, and sprinkle with chopped walnuts, cinnamon and sesame. Leave to cool, and serve as it is or cut into portions.

5 kg grape must
4 cups flour
½ kg potash
Walnuts
Cinnamon

Isli

Prepare the filling by mixing all the ingredients together. Then mix the oil with the sugar and slowly add the flour which you have previously mixed with the salt and baking powder. Form a dough by adding water until a soft mass is achieved. Take pieces of the mixture about the size of a walnut, make a hole in the centre of each with your finger and put in 1 tsp of the filling. Close the dough well around the filling and place them on an oiled baking sheet with the join downwards. Bake at 200 C for about 50 minutes, until they are browned. Meanwhile, prepare the syrup by mixing all the ingredients together and letting them boil for about 5 minutes. Let the syrup cool and then pour it over the 'isli' when you take them out of the oven.

2 cups oil
1 cup of water
2 tbs sugar
Pinch of salt
1 little envelope of baking powder
1 kg flour

Filling:
1 ½ cups chopped walnuts
2-3 cloves, ground
2 tsp cinnamon
2 tbs sugar

Syrup:
1 cup sugar
1 cup honey
1 ½ cups of water
½ cup cognac

Little mandarin oranges

Rub the mandarin oranges a little on a grater, then peel them. Boil the peel in a large among of water, then empty the water away, add fresh water and continue to boil until they have softened well. Drain, then mash them to pulp. Pound the almonds in a mortar. Add the sugar and the juice of the mandarins to the pan and let it boil a couple of times. Before the mixture thickens, add the pulp and, finally, the almonds. Beat well with a wooden spoon and as soon as the mixture has thickened and draws away from the sides of the pan, remove it from the heat. Leave it to cool, then form it into balls and roll them in crystallized sugar.

(If the mixture does not thicken well and cannot be formed into balls, add more almonds or breadcrumbs)

4 mandarin oranges
320 gr sugar
320 gr almonds (shelled)
Crystallised sugar

'Vrahakia'
('little rocks')

Melt the chocolate in a bain-marie and add the almonds. Take spoonfuls of the mixture and drop them onto greaseproof paper. Leave for several hours to set. When they are ready, they can be wrapped in cellophane or aluminium foil.

1 kg chocolate for
cake covering

800 gr whole
shelled almonds

Kourambiedes

Beat the oil and sugar well together in a bowl. Add the baking soda, lemon, walnuts, and finally the flour in stages, to make a fairly firm dough. Form into shapes, either round or whatever you prefer, and place them on a lightly oiled baking tin.
Bake in a preheated oven for about 40 minutes. When they are ready, remove from the heat and sprinkle over a little flower water, then dust them thickly with powdered sugar (use a sieve).

1 kg flour
2 tbs sugar
3 tbs chopped
walnuts
½ tsp baking soda
½ lemon (juice and
zest required)
½ kg powdered
sugar
Flower water
2 cups oil

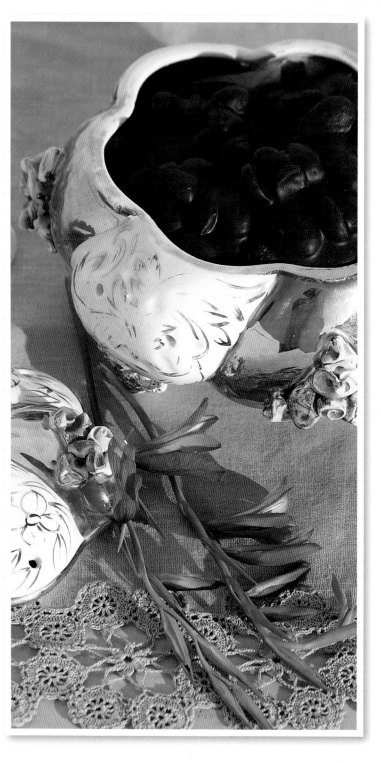

Sámali

Put the semolina, sugar, baking powder and orange and lemon zest into a bowl. Slowly add the liquid ingredients, i.e. the orange juice and water, and stir well with a spoon. Butter a baking dish well and pour the mixture into it. Bake in the oven at 200 C for about ¾ of an hour. Meanwhile, prepare the syrup by boiling the sugar and the water together in a saucepan with the orange peel.

When the sámali has baked, remove it from the oven, score it diagonally and pour over the syrup. It is a good idea to leave the dish for one day in the syrup, so that it can be thoroughly absorbed.

3 cups semolina
1 cup sugar
1 cup orange juice
1 cup water
5 tbs baking powder
Lemon and orange zest

Syrup:
2 cups sugar
3 cups water
(or 2 cups of water + 1 cup of orange juice)
Orange peel

'Saraglákia', from Xánthi

Start by making the syrup: Place the water, sugar and lemon juice in a saucepan and leave to boil until a light syrup has formed. Remove the syrup from the heat and leave it to cool. Beat the eggs and powdered sugar well together, using a mixer. Add the melted butter and, slowly, the flour, into which you have mixed the baking powder and salt. Finally, add the semolina and knead to form a medium dough. Form into little balls, press their surfaces slightly flat and place an almond in each. Place the balls in a buttered dish and bake at 180 C for about 40 minutes. As soon as they brown, remove them from the oven and pour over the syrup which, in the meantime, will have cooled.

180 gr powdered sugar
2 eggs
250 gr unsalted butter
2 1/2 cups flour
1 level tbs baking powder
1/2 tsp salt
180 gr semolina
50 skinned almonds

Syrup:
4 cups sugar
3 cups water
1 tsp lemon juice

Semolina halva

Heat the oil in a pan and add the semolina. Mix well until the semolina begins to roast and take on a dark brown colour. In another pan, boil the water with the sugar, stirring it for about 5 minutes until the sugar has dissolved and then add the lemon zest. When the syrup is ready add it slowly to the pan containing the halva, and let it boil for a little while until the semolina has absorbed it. At the same time, add the almonds. Cover the halva with a clean tea towel and let it cool. Serve dusted with the cinnamon.

1 cup semolina
1/2 cup oil
100 gr blanched almonds
cinnamon

Syrup:
1 1/2 cups sugar
2 1/2 cups of water
Zest of a lemon

Fresh walnut spoon sweet

Skin the walnuts, wash them and boil them until they are soft. Then put them in a pan with fresh water and change it every eight hours over the space of two days. When the walnuts have lost their bitterness, boil the sugar with the water for 10 minutes and add the walnuts and the almonds to boil in the syrup for about 7 minutes. Turn off the heat and leave the walnuts to stand in their syrup for a day. Then, replace the pan on the heat and boil until the syrup has thickened well. Finally, add the lemon juice, let the mixture boil for 5 minutes and the spoon sweet is ready.

1 ½ kg fresh walnuts
1 ½ kg blanched almonds
1 ½ kg sugar
3 cups of water
1 glass of lemon juice

Sour cherry spoon sweet

Wash the cherries and remove the stones, using a special instrument if you have one. Spread them out in a pan in alternate layers with the sugar. Leave for about 2-3 hours and then add the water and boil until the mixture thickens.

When it is ready, add the lemon; after cooling, pour into glass jars and store in a cool place.

1 kg sour cherries
1 ½ kg sugar
1 cup of water
1 tsp lemon

Sour cherry drink

Cut off the stalks of the cherries, wash them and remove the stones. Puree them in a blender. Place the puree in a fine sieve and press out all the juice; boil it with the lemon juice and the sugar until a thickish syrup is obtained, as in spoon sweets. When it is ready, allow to cool and then pour into clean, dry bottles.

1 kg sour cherries
1 kg sugar
Juice of 1 lemon

Cherry
spoon sweet

1 kg cherries,
1 kg sugar,
½ cup water

Select firm cherries which will withstand boiling. Remove the stalks, wash the cherries and dry them with a cloth. Put the sugar and water into a pan, turn on the heat and as soon as the sugar has dissolved (without letting it boil) add the cherries. Now bring them to the boil once or twice and remove from the heat. When they have cooled, remove the fruit from the pan with a slotted spoon and put them on a plate. Then return the syrup to the heat and boil it until it is well thickened. Add the cherries again and bring to the boil a couple of times. Add a little lemon juice and remove the pan from the heat. When the spoon sweet is cold, pour it into clean jars.

Quince spoon sweet

Take large quinces, rub them on a sieve and
cut them into small strips. Put them into a
pan with the water and bring to the boil a
couple of times, until they soften.

Add the sugar and boil over a high heat,
until the syrup forms, taking care that the
quinces retain their yellow colour and do
not redden. Finally, add the lemon juice
and after boiling for a few minutes, remove
from the heat and add the almonds.

1 kg quinces
1 kg sugar
2 cups of water
1 tsp lemon
juice
½ cup
blanched
almonds

Little pear spoon sweet

2 kg small pears
2 kg sugar
4 lemons
As many almonds as pears

Wash the pears, peel them and cut off the stems. Remove the pips carefully, so that each fruit remains in one piece. Put the pears in a bowl of cold water and add the juice of two lemons. Place an almond inside every pear. Now put them into a pan, add water to half cover them, and half of the sugar.

Let them boil and then add the remaining sugar and the juice of 2 lemons. Continue boiling until the syrup has formed. Turn off the heat, allow them to cool a little and fill them into jars.

Orange spoon sweet

Rub the oranges on a grater and then remove their peel in vertical sections. Score the oranges vertically and remove the peel from the oranges.

Wind the peel into rolls and secure them with toothpicks. Now boil the rolls for 5 minutes, change the water, boil them again and strain them.

Put the sugar into a pan with 2 litres of water and boil it until the syrup is almost formed. Then, add the rolls of orange peel and leave them to simmer for 15 minutes until the syrup is thick.

10 oranges
1 kg sugar

Small aubergine spoon sweet

Wash the aubergines, cut off the stalks and make an incision along the length of each. Place them in water for 24 hours, changing the water every 8 hours.

When they have sweetened, drain off the water; insert two almonds into each incision and push a clove into the top of each aubergine. Boil the sugar with the water, cinnamon and a few cloves for 5 minutes. Add the aubergines and boil for another 5 minutes. Turn off the heat and leave the aubergines in the syrup for 24 hours. Afterwards, bring to the boil again over a high heat, remove the scum, add the lemon and let it boil once or twice again to thicken up the syrup.

1 kg small aubergines

1 ½ kg sugar

½ kg blanched almonds

2 sticks cinnamon

Whole cloves

1 tsp lemon juice

2 cups of water

Grape spoon sweet

Remove the stalks from the grapes, which should be selected for their freshness and firmness. Wash them, and put them into a pan in alternate layers with the sugar. Leave them for one night so that the moisture exudes from the fruit and the sugar dissolves.

Next day, boil the mixture until the sugar has completely dissolved and a syrup has formed. Finally, add the geranium leaves, let the mixture boil for a short while again and then remove it from the heat. When it is cold, pour it into clean jars to store.

1 kg sultana grapes
1 kg sugar
2-3 leaves of sweet geranium (Pelargonium odoratissimum)

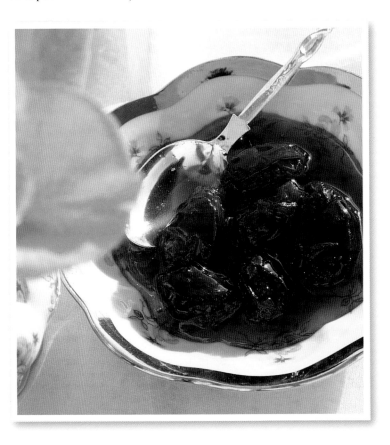

Bitter orange spoon sweet

Wash the oranges, dry them and rub them on a grater to take off a little of their surfaces. Place them in cold water. Score them vertically and take off the peel in sections. Take each piece of peel separately and wind it into a roll with the white pith on the inside; thread all the rolls onto a string, using a thick needle. Tie the ends so that they cannot unthread. Boil them in a large amount of water until they soften. Now place them in cold water and leave for a whole day, changing the water 3 or 4 times so that the peel loses its bitterness. Drain well and lay the string on a cloth to drain further. Place them in a pan and cover them with 1 cup of sugar and 1 cup of water. Bring to the boil and, shortly before the syrup begins to form, remove the string. Continue boiling until the spoon sweet is ready. Allow to cool and pack into clean, dry jars.

1 kg bitter oranges
1 kg sugar

Plum jam

Wash the plums and remove the stones. Cut them into pieces and place in a pan with the sugar and a very small amount of water. Boil at first over a low heat and then raise the temperature, stirring the mixture constantly with a wooden spoon. The jam has set when a quantity is lifted out of the pan on a wooden spoon, then emptied back into it, and a layer of jam is seen to remain on the spoon. Then add the lemon juice, stir and remove from the heat. Pour the hot jam into jars and cover when it has cooled.

2 kg plums
2 ½ kg sugar
1 lemon

Apricot marmalade

Choose firm, ripe apricots. Wash them
well, cut them up and remove the stones.
Put them in a pan with one cup of water
and boil them until they have softened
and become a puree.

Process them in your blender, to ensure
that no pieces of skin have remained,
and put the puree back into the
saucepan with the sugar. Boil, stirring
well with a wooden spoon so that the mixture does not stick to
the bottom of the pan.

The marmalade has set if it coats the back of a spoon and stays
there when held downwards. Now add the lemon juice. Let it boil
once or twice again and then remove the pan from the heat. Pour
the marmalade, when cold, into clean, dry jars.

1 kg apricots
1 kg sugar
1 tsp lemon juice
1 cup of water

BREAD
&
'PAXIMADIA'
(RUSKS)

Bread made with sourdough

The evening before, 'restart' the sourdough by adding 1 kg flour and a little water to make a very soft dough (it should, however, not be runny). Put it into a bowl and cover it with ½ kg flour. Now place the bowl in a plastic bag, close it well and cover it with a warm cloth.

Next day, when the mixture is well risen, add the remaining flour, oil, salt and, very slowly, water so that the mixture takes on the appearance of 'mastiha' (gum).

2 ½ kg flour
(1½ kg wholemeal and 1 kg white)

½ cup oil

3 tsp salt

1 cup sourdough

After kneading the dough very well for quite a while and periodically wetting your hands, form it into loaves (round or elongated), wrap them with a clean cotton or linen tea towel and place a blanket on top. Leave to rise in a warm place. After about 3-4 hours, when the bread is well risen, place them on a (preferably) metal baking tray lined with greaseproof paper.

Bake in a preheated oven, at first at 180 C and then at 200 C, for about one hour.

If liked, sunflower seeds, pine nuts, raisins, olives etc. can be added to the bread.

Lagana

Dissolve the yeast in a little warm water, mix it well with a little flour to form a thick cream and leave it in a warm place to bubble.

Put the flour into a bowl and make a well in the centre; add the oil, sugar, salt, yeast and a little warm water.

Mix together, adding warm water at intervals, until a dough is obtained; it should not be sticky. Form it into a ball, cover it with a cotton cloth and leave it in a warm place to rise.

When the dough is ready, cut small pieces and roll out each to an oval with a thickness of ½ cm. Place them on an oiled dish, cover again with a cloth, and leave to rise. Finally, push your fingers into the surface to form little holes, brush with oil, sprinkle over the sesame, and bake in a moderate oven until they are browned.

1 kg flour
2 tsp fresh yeast
2 tbs sugar
1 cup oil
1 tsp salt
Sesame
Warm water

Sweet rusks made with sourdough

'Restart' the sourdough by kneading it with ¾ kg of flour and a little water. Leave overnight to rise. The next morning, mix it to a dough with the other ingredients, apart from the sesame. Form elongated loaves and cut them them vertically into slices, so that you can separate the paximadia from one another later. Scatter the sesame over a tray or work surface and roll the loaves in it. Cover and leave in a warm place to rise. When the loaves are ready, bake them at first in a moderate oven (180 C) and then increase the temperature. As soon as they have browned, turn off the heat and leave them to cool. They can be eaten when they are soft. If liked, however, they can be dried and hardened by returning them to the oven at a low heat, until all the moisture has evaporated and they become crunchy.

3 kg flour
700 gr sugar
3 cups oil
300 gr sesame
½ a little bottle of cinnamon oil
2 tsp ground cloves
2 tsp mastiha
100 gr coriander
1 tsp cinnamon
1 tsp pepper
Sourdough (about 1 cup)

Rusks with raisins

Beat the sugar and the oil and add the orange and cinnamon juices (make the latter by boiling 2-3 cinnamon sticks in water). Now add the ammonia, clove, cinnamon, raisins, almonds and the flour mixed with the baking powder. Mix well to a dough with your hands and form into long sticks. Score them deeply and vertically with a knife to form slices and bake in a moderate oven until they brown. When you take them from the oven, separate off the slices and then put them on a baking dish. Return to the oven at a low temperature, until all the moisture has evaporated and they become crunchy.

1 cup oil
1 cup sugar
1 cup raisins
1 cup almonds
1 cup orange juice
1 cup cinnamon juice
½ cup flour
1 tsp cinnamon
1 tsp clove
1 envelope ammonia
1 envelope baking powder